"An Artist Is His Own Fault"

John O'Hara

on Writers and Writing

Edited with an Introduction by
Matthew J. Bruccoli
Jefferies Professor of English
University of South Carolina

Southern Illinois University Press
Carbondale and Edwardsville

Feffer & Simons, Inc.
London and Amsterdam

Copyright © 1977 by United States Trust Company
  of New York as trustee under the will of John O'Hara
Introduction by Matthew J. Bruccoli, Copyright © 1976 by
  Southern Illinois University Press
All rights reserved
Printed in the United States of America
Designed by Gary Gore

Library of Congress Cataloging in Publication Data

O'Hara, John, 1905–1970.
    "An artist is his own fault."

    1.   O'Hara, John, 1905–1970—Technique—Addresses,
essays, lectures.   2.   Fiction—Technique—
Addresses, essays, lectures.   I.   Bruccoli, Matthew
Joseph, 1931–   II.   Title.
PS3529.H29Z78   1977   813'.5'2   76–43279
ISBN 0–8093–0796–0

To Peter Shepherd of
Harold Ober Associates

Contents

Book Reviews and Reading Lists

Interviews and Public Statements

Introduction

by Matthew J. Bruccoli

The qualities that the critics consistently recognized in John O'Hara's work were his "ear for speech" and his "eye for detail"—as though his ear and eye were connected directly to a typewriter. There has been a disinclination to grant O'Hara his stature as an artist because he made his art seem too easy, and his high level of productivity has been adduced as evidence that he was a careless writer. It is true that he was deficient in certain kinds of craftsmanship. His refusal to revise in the latter period of his career is worrisome: his first draft was the only draft. Any work of literature can be improved, and we admire authors who revise successive layers of their work in the attempt to meet interior standards of perfection. But O'Hara prided himself on what he called "pre-paper discipline," and he believed that he knew exactly what he wanted to do before he touched his typewriter. The purpose of this volume is to reveal the scope and level of O'Hara's thinking about his craft—which was also his profession. The concept of professionalism defines O'Hara's approach to his work. He believed that a professional was someone who had mastered his craft, who wrote steadily, and who consistently achieved a high level of work.

John O'Hara published no organized body of literary criticism, scattering his critical ideas in the columns he wrote for *Newsweek*, the *Trenton Times-Advertiser*, *Collier's*, *Long Island Newsday*, and *Holiday*. Yet there is abundant evidence—in his fiction as well as in his comments on writers and writing—that he thought hard about the craft of fiction and the profession of authorship. He said of F. Scott Fitzgerald, "an artist is his own fault." So is his contemporary reputation. O'Hara antagonized the opinion-makers and prize-givers. Although he openly sought recognition, his usual response to an award was "What the hell took you so long?"

It is a truism that when writers write about writing, they write about their own work. Their shop-talk is often superb; it is stimulating to hear professionals discuss the skills they have mastered. John O'Hara on the subject of writers and writing is worth while for at least two good reasons: it enlarges our understanding of O'Hara's own craftsmanship, and it reveals a great deal about the profession of authorship during the forty years he practiced it.

This volume would merit publication if it included only the three previously unpublished Rider College Lectures. In these lectures, delivered in 1959 and 1961 when O'Hara was at the peak of his powers, we have his major critical statement—his only attempt to formalize his thinking about the techniques of fiction. The Rider Lectures are particularly useful because they are developed with close reference to his own work—not in generalities. They are a master's attempt to reveal the lessons he had learned and the rules he had formulated for his own work.

At Rider, O'Hara—a man of legendary testiness— addressed himself to two of the labels that had been applied to him by critics: that he was a social historian, and that he practiced the *roman à clef*. He properly felt that these labels were patronizing. Consequently his remarks are defensive. Perhaps too defensive, for he uses the term *social fiction* in a special way so as to dissociate himself from it. Surprisingly, in the 1959 lectures he plays down the importance of social history as an element of literary art, perhaps because it was one of the *mere*-terms that were applied to his work by critics who like their fiction relevant and committed: mere social history, mere surface realism, mere detail, mere reportage, mere accuracy of speech. Although O'Hara manifested contempt for critics, in 1959 he was hurt by the reviews of *From the Terrace* (1958)—the novel he considered his greatest work—which complained about needless piling up of social detail.

In the 1960 introduction to *Sermons and Soda-Water* O'Hara offered this credo: "The United States in this century is what I know, and it is my business to write about it to the best of my ability, with the sometimes special knowledge I have. The twenties, the thirties, and the forties are already history, but I cannot be content to leave their story in the hands of the historians and the editors of picture books. I want to record the way people talked and thought and felt, and to do it with complete honesty and variety." But a year earlier at Rider he had stated, "Social history has absolutely no standing in the world of art as I see it." And in 1961: "I deny that I am a social historian; I am a novelist, and a social historian only incidentally. Nevertheless my novels do partake of the elements and classification of social history, and behind my decision to make a novel is the question, can I say what I want to say about my times as well as what I want to say about my people, my characters?" He believed that writers who set out to write social history are usually working in accordance with some socio-political doctrine or are trying to study a social problem. Consequently, they are more concerned with forces than with characters, with problems rather than with psychology. In his novels the creation of characters—not social history—was O'Hara's greatest consideration. But he was using the term "social history" in a special way. The distinction should be made between *social fiction* (the novel of manners) and *sociological fiction* (the problem novel). John O'Hara was our greatest novelist of manners, and he had a total commitment to social verisimilitude.* Neither as a young liberal nor as an old conservative did he write about social problems. He wrote one political allegory, *The Farmers Hotel* (1951), in which the characters were so convincing and the social documentation so thorough—and the allegory so concealed—that it was not recognized as such.

O'Hara's main concern in his Rider lectures was with character creation—with the problems of making characters believable, and with the greater problem of creating a character who would carry a novel. Here again O'Hara tried to refute a standard comment on his work—that his characters were copies of real people, that he practiced the *roman à clef*. Only *Butterfield 8* is a *roman à clef*. In none of his other novels is there this simple relationship between real-life person and fictional character. His other characters are composites of the psychological pattern of one real person—not the actual behavior, but the psychological pattern—and the "superficial characteristics" of at least one other person. This is how he created Joe Chapin of *Ten North Frederick*: "In that instance I took a real person whose life was rather dramatically changed by an episode that made a tremendous difference in his mode of living. The episode occurred when my real-life person was a grown man, and a man set in his ways. Now what I, the novelist, did was to pretend that the dramatic episode—over which, by the way, he had no control—had never occurred. What kind of man would this be, how would he have turned out, if the episode had not occurred? From then on I wrote pure fiction." No one identified this real-life man, who—and O'Hara did not reveal this in his

---

*The term "novel of manners" is somehow unsatisfactory for American Literature; it suggests the English novel and the English class-structure. Perhaps a new term is needed for the kind of novel Lewis, Marquand, and Tarkington wrote—and O'Hara wrote better than anyone else. "The recording novel" has been proposed, but that is too open-ended.

lectures—was Franklin Delano Roosevelt. *Ten North Frederick* is not a *roman à clef* about President Roosevelt, because it does not actually use real people or real events. O'Hara provided no clues to the connection between Chapin and Roosevelt, for the connection does not matter to the reader. The novel derived from the author's analysis of the psychology of a real person—which is not at all the same thing as a *roman à clef*. The O'Hara method of character creation is more complicated than it appears. Note that while insisting that he did not write the *roman à clef*—in his novels, anyhow—he still insists that his created characters must be true to their real-life models. It could be argued that O'Hara was writing a greatly modified *roman à clef* with special controls. Although the regular *roman à clef* is based on more or less disguised real people and disguised real events, the author sticks close to them and expects at least some readers to find the key. John O'Hara created true-to-life composites that were not supposed to be recognized: the *roman à clef* sans the clef.

When O'Hara discussed the creation of believable characters, he did so in terms of social accuracy. Character emerges from speech, and speech is governed by the speaker's social-economic-educational background. Dialogue must seem real, and one wrong word may destroy the characterization for a reader—who may not even be aware of just what is wrong. Here O'Hara is in the difficulty that has been encountered by every realistic-naturalistic writer. Real speech cannot be duplicated in print, and no writer has ever seriously tried it. O'Hara admits this impossibility and thereby tacitly admits that his superbly real dialogue is artificial. He doesn't write what people actually say; he contrives a controlled impression of the vocabulary, grammar, and rhythms. It is worth stating the obvious because so much condescending praise has been given to John O'Hara's "tape-recorder ear"—which implies that his dialogue is reportage.

Related to the details of speech are other social details, which O'Hara insists are significant details. Even the wrong details must be deliberately and therefore significantly wrong. O'Hara expects a good reader to recognize there is something fraudulent about a character who wears a tyrolean hat with a chesterfield. Details function as characterizers. One of O'Hara's favorite characterizers was the automobile—see his discussion of the Franklin. Note well that he is talking about the Franklin as a characterizer, not simply as a class symbol. It is revealing that this example is set in the twenties, for many of the characterizers O'Hara used so brilliantly no longer exist. The Franklin is gone, and so are the other cars in its class. Men's clothes haven't worked well as a characterizer for at least a decade. Remember, John O'Hara applied the adjective "superficial" to these details of social verisimilitude. He prided himself on the psychological truth of his created characters. The proof that his characters—not their possessions—do carry his novels is provided by the fact that his books have been read by millions of people who never heard of the Franklin or Spitalsfield ties or Peal shoes or the Racquet Club or Skull and Bones or Brooks Brothers.

The rest of this volume has been assembled from published and unpublished material with the intention of giving an impression of the range—both of subject and occasion—of O'Hara's statements on his craft. At least two more of the previously unpublished pieces are valuable additions to the O'Hara canon: the foreword to *The Selected Stories of John O'Hara* ("These Stories Were Part of Me") and "Characters in Search." It is difficult to avoid the grab-bag approach in preparing a volume like this one; the editor has not been particularly concerned about avoiding it. The editorial plan has been to assemble O'Hara's most useful statements about writers and writing—omitting his introductions to his volumes of stories, which are widely available.

The following previously unpublished pieces in the Estate of John O'Hara are published with the generous permission of Carter, Ledyard & Milburn and The United States Trust Co.: The Rider College Lectures, "These Stories Were Part of Me," "I Was Determined to Make Plain what I Had Seen," "Characters in Search," "My Favorite Room." Grateful acknowledgment is made to the following libraries for these previously unpublished pieces: Collection of American Literature, The Beinecke Rare Book and Manuscript Library, Yale University for "Writing—What's in it for Me?"; Rutgers University Library for "What Makes a Writer?"; the Pennsylvania State University Libraries for "The Prize is a Good One" and "We All Know how Good We Are."

Special acknowledgments are made to Wylie O'Hara Doughty, to Theodore Wagner and Peter P. McN. Gates of Carter, Ledyard & Milburn, and to Henry Heil of The United States Trust Co. I am permanently indebted to Charles Mann, Curator of Rare Books and Special Collections at the Pennsylvania State University Libraries, the able caretaker of the John O'Hara Papers.

The Rider College Lectures

✍ Foreword

Rider College is a nonsectarian, coeducational institution that began in 1865 as Trenton Business College, in 1919 adopted the name Rider after Andrew J. Rider, one of the founders, and in 1959 invited me to lecture on the Novel. Novelists get those invitations all the time, and I accept very few of them; but there were two things about the Rider invitation that made me consider, and then accept. One was that I would be the first novelist to participate in the new Liberal Arts program at Rider; the other was that the invitation was put to me as a neighbor of Rider. Since I had recently completed work on a novel and had not yet started work on my next, I consented to give the two lectures that make up this book. For me it was as pleasant an experience as lecturing can ever be, and I take this opportunity to thank the men and women at Rider who helped make it a pleasant experience, and to wish the College every success in its ambitious new Liberal Arts program.

J. O'H.

12 November 1959
Princeton, New Jersey

1 ✒ Dialog, Detail, and Type

I naturally assume that men and women who will come out at this hour to hear an American novelist's lectures on the American Novel are seriously interested in the subject. I therefore shall take for granted that you have done a fair amount of reading of the novels of my contemporaries and of the novels I have written. Indeed, it is quite probable that you have read more novels than I have in recent years. In spite of the best of intentions I still have not read *By Love Possessed*, although I admire James Gould Cozzens; and I have read only a few pages of *Dr. Zhivago*, although I know I ought really to. My excuse for my neglect of these outstanding novels of recent years is that I am a very slow reader of fiction, and a sort of subexcuse is that because of my slowness I cannot afford the time while I am in the most productive period of my professional life.

I read slowly because when I read a novel I am intently busy. It sometimes takes me half an hour to read a page, because I read first for the story, such as it may be, and then I go back over the page to see how the author got his effects, if he got them; or why he failed, if he did not get them. I distrust all figures of speech, and you should too, because they are incompletely accurate and ultimately undependable, but when I read a novel I am something like a composer listening to another composer's phonograph records. I feel reasonably sure, for example, that George Gershwin, when he was composing *A Rhapsody*

John O'Hara gave two lectures to a class on the American novel at Rider College in 1959. A third lecture was delivered in 1961. Although he thought well enough of the first two lectures to have considered publication and wrote a foreword for them, none of the three saw print. The lectures are published from the typescripts in the Estate of John O'Hara. The titles for the lectures have been supplied by the editor.

in Blue, listened over and over again to Darius Milhaud's
Creation of the World; and before the phonograph was
invented earlier composers surely played Bach and Paganini again and again and then sat over in a corner and
studied the Bach and Paganini scores. I can remember
that when I was in my teens I was always paying fines—
two cents a day—because I owed the Public Library for
books I had kept out too long. If I have any debt to John
Galsworthy it is not a monetary one; I shelled out the price
of a pack of cigarettes often enough to have a clear conscience on that. And in passing I might mention that eight
or nine years ago, when I was a long way from my teens, I
had to pay the Firestone Library $35 for some books I had
kept out too long. They were in French.

You may want to ask what I look for, what kind of thing
I look for, when I go plodding through a novel by one of
my contemporaries. That would be a helpful question, so
I hope you do want to ask it. I also hope I can answer it,
and I'll try. Let me start with the most obvious example,
which is dialog.

I have been told often enough that I write the best
dialog that is being written. I make this immodest statement because many of my critics seem to feel that they
have to say, or strongly imply, that my gift for dialog is all
I have; or that writing dialog is not the most important
attribute a novelist can have. Well, it is *not* the most
essential part of an author's equipment. The basic, indispensable attribute of a novelist is the understanding of
character and the ability to create characters, and they go
together, since understanding without creation means no
novel and no novelist. But I discovered when I was very
young, before I was in my teens, that nothing could so
quickly cast doubt on, and even destroy, an author's
characters as bad dialog. If the people did not talk right,
they were not real people. The closer to real talk, the closer
to real people, and forty years ago the dialog in the books I

read was not very real. Two more or less local men—Booth Tarkington, of Princeton, and Owen Johnson, of the Lawrenceville stories—wrote dialog that I liked better than the dialog I was then reading in short stories and serials in the *American Boy*. Of course I did not take into account the fact that Tarkington and Johnson were not writing for boys of cub scout age, or that most readers of the *American Boy*, including the present speaker, were more interested in action, plot development, than in the verisimilitude of speech. I cannot and would not claim that when I was eleven years old I lingered appreciatively over the spoken words of Penrod Schofield, but it is obvious this evening that Tarkington and Johnson made more of an impression on me than the men who wrote for the *American Boy*. And the reason they did is not so much that they wrote good dialog as that they were better writers; the dialog was only one part of their better writing.

A man or woman who does not write good dialog is not a first-rate writer.

I do not believe that a writer who neglects or has not learned to write good dialog can be depended upon for accuracy in his understanding of character and his creation of characters. Therefore to dismiss good dialog so lightly is evidence of a critic's incomplete understanding of what constitutes a good novel. I think I was the first to use the expression, a tin ear, in connection with the writing of bad dialog. The tin ear has always meant the inability to carry a tune, but an author who has a tin ear is one who forces his characters to say things they would not say, in ways they would not say it; and most authors have tin ears. This would not be so bad if it was an isolated fault, but it seldom is. Let me give you an example.

Some years ago, when I was writing a great many short stories for a magazine, I was called in by an editor to discuss a story in which one of the characters was an upper-class New York girl, a Spence-Chapin-Brearley type girl. I had given this girl a line of dialog which went something like this: "Robert didn't come with she and I." I repeat the line: "Robert didn't come with she and I." Now obviously the girl should have said "with her and me." The preposition *with* governing the objective case. The editor, a college graduate and a Junior League type herself, maintained that the girl would not have made the grammatical mistake I had her make. But the editor was an editor and not an author, and she had never written any dialog. She was also, let's face it, a bit of a snob, and she was trying to tell me that people like her did not make such mistakes. My point, however, was that just such a mistake was made all the time, and that it revealed more about the girl than a hundred words of descriptive matter. Girls who went to fashionable schools would not say, "Josephine is prettier than me." They would have had drummed into them the rule that the verb to be takes the same case after it as before it, and they would go through life correctly saying, "Josephine is prettier than I." But while learning that one rule they also were developing what might be called an elegant resistance of the objective pronouns. I therefore stubbornly refused to make the change that the editor suggested, and the story appeared as I had written it. The incident had a happy ending. A few weeks later I saw the editor again and she said to me: "You were right about *she and I.* They say it all the time, even my niece says it." Well, I knew that, or I wouldn't have written *she and I,* but I was pleased that I had been able to teach an editor to listen for the peculiarities of speech that occur in all classes. Whenever an author can teach an editor anything he has not only done himself a favor, but he has just possibly made it a little easier for other authors.

This theory of mine, that I could be persuaded to call O'Hara's Law, that an author who does not write good dialog is not a first-rate author—is not something I stumbled on, or arrived at overnight. I have indicated earlier that a line of bad dialog can destroy a character, even for the nonprofessional reader who does not know why the character has become unbelievable. I discovered O'Hara's Law in my own laboratory. I love to write. When I am not writing I am really wasting my time, and when I no longer can write, I will soon die. Now one of the many experiments I have conducted in my laboratory—and I hope you realize that I am not being serious when I refer to it as my laboratory—is to put a sheet of paper in the typewriter, think of two faces I have seen, make up a scene, such as a restaurant table or two seats in an airplane, and get those two people into conversation. I let them do small talk for a page or two, and pretty soon they begin to come to life. They do so entirely through dialog. I start by knowing nothing about them except what I remember of their faces. But as they chatter away, one of them, and then the other, will say something that is so revealing that I recognize the signs of created characters. From then on it is a question of how deeply I want to interest myself in the characters. If I become absorbed in the characters, I can write a novel about them and so can any other novelist. A fine novel can be written about any two people in the world—by a first-rate novelist. A great novel could be written about any man or woman that ever lived—by a great novelist. But while I have written, and published, short stories that had such accidental beginnings, I do not approach the writing of novels in such casual fashion. As a rule I don't even finish the stories I begin that way, and I deliberately destroy what I have done by giving one of the characters a line of atrocious dialog—humorous, profane, or completely out of character—that makes it impossible seriously to continue. I have killed an hour between the Jack Paar show and bedtime, and I have not been alone.

As serious students of the novel you have often read reviews in which the author is credited, if that's quite the word, with having a phonographic ear. Nowadays they say tape-recorder ear. That is supposed to be complimentary, that the author writes such good dialog that he is suspected of getting help from the magic world of electronics. I have no way of estimating how much harm that cliché may have done to young writers, not to mention how much money their poor fathers may have spent in the actual purchase of tape recording apparatus. A writer, young or old, who must depend on tape recording to catch real speech had better stop wasting his time and the old man's money, while there is still hope that he can find some useful occupation. The writing of dialog really cannot be learned and cannot be taught. You have the gift, or you haven't. If you have the gift, you can refine it and improve on it and learn to handle it, but the absence of it is like tone deafness or the inability to mimic people. I flunked trigonometry, and I'm not ashamed to admit it. So I did not become a mathematician. On the other hand, I have a good ear for music; in the privacy of the home I am a fairly good mimic; and I write good dialog, without resorting to any mechanical or electrical apparatus. Moreover, the dialog I write in my novels and short stories is always under my control. Always. If you are interested in tape-recorded dialog, which is a good study for a writer or any nonwriter who would care to read pure speech, pure in the sense that it is put down exactly as spoken, I suggest you look in your New York newspapers any Thursday morning, and read the transcripts of the White House press conference of the day before; or, if you want to go to a little more trouble, get the transcripts of any court trials here in Trenton. You will then begin to understand why I say that I keep my dialog always under control. You will learn, for instance, that in ordinary conversation practically no one ever finishes a sentence. This is not the fault of the interrupters. It is chronic with nearly everybody. As a young newspaper reporter I discovered this great truth, simply by taking notes. I knew short-hand, because I was too young to go away to school when I finished eighth grade, and so I was kept home and took the commercial course, the only course available in the parochial school in those days. I never made much use of my shorthand, except now and then to take down the speech of some brilliant orator for my own amusement. If I had quoted him verbatim he would have sued the paper. Quote any man verbatim for five minutes of extem-poraneous speech and you will let him make an ass of himself. If you have absolute faith in the system of trial by jury, don't read any court trial transcripts. You will be terribly disillusioned to find that what the lawyers have said during a trial makes no sense when it is reduced to the printed word, and even in capital cases the judge's charge to the jury is in all probability so much gibberish. As for social conversation, if you do happen to have a tape recorder, you can embarrass yourself and your friends by playing back the recording of the most serious discus-sions. It is simply amazing to find how little communica-tion depends on the things we actually say.

Now this is something that most authors never, never learn, and they don't learn it because they are unaware of the importance of dialog. Dialog is used, by someone who knows how to use it, in creating and maintaining charac-ter, in advancing a story, and in giving life to a scene. But tape-recorded dialog would do neither. It is one thing to admit or claim that I write credible conversations, naturalistic speech. But it is something else to say I have a phonographic ear. My dialog is good because I never allow a character to say anything he would not say, that is not a product of his social and educational background and of the occasion on which he is speaking, relaxed, under stress, drunk, sober, tired, or whatever the occa-sion may be. But most importantly his social, that is to say his social and economic background, and his educational background govern the way he expresses himself in words. Well-educated men and women—and I have listened to them in high society and in parties at the Institute for Advanced Study—disobey the ordinary· rules of grammar whenever they open their mouths, and they do not speak in sentences. They do have better vocabularies than the uneducated or the less well educated, and they finish their thoughts. But if you have ever taken a taxi from Penn Station to Grand Central you have had to listen to a taxi driver finishing his thought, whatever it may be—usually his idea of how to solve the traffic problem or the conduct of the United Nations or the way he would run the Yankees in 1960. So perhaps I am overemphasizing the virtue of finishing a thought, and should only make the point that the great brain at an Institute party expresses himself more graciously than the hackie, and a good dialog writer can create the speech of both convincingly, without using a tape recorder.

Control of dialog by an author means not only his getting the speech down so that it seems real. Control also can be useful in other ways. For instance, in the writing of a scene between a man and woman who are parting after a love affair it may be the author's intention to create a mood of sadness, grief at the prospect of parting, but without getting maudlin. Here the author can make his man and woman talk away for a couple of pages, saying the homely, ordinary things that make up the most of human speech. But he can stretch out the conversation, if he has complete control, so that just the length of the conversation and the banality of it can convey a sense of the agonizing experience the two people are going through. He must know precisely where to end it, and God knows he must know where to begin. Later on I am going to take up the hypnotic effect of type, to demonstrate how effectively type can be used in subtly influencing the reader, but for the moment I only want to point out that the quick, short sentences that would appear in such a scene as I have described are part of an author's control of dialog that goes beyond his editing of the words.

No one but the author should ever be permitted to do any editing of his words. It is a pity that we have now reached the point where this or that pressure group can be strong enough to censor or influence the writing of dialog. One of the funniest men I ever read was Milt Gross, but his Nize Baby pieces would now be rejected on the curious ground of bad taste. Arthur Kober once told me that he got many abusive letters from other Jews for his mild and tender pieces about the Bronx characters he created. Last year I was angered and dismayed to read that Pearl Bailey, of all people, had taken upon herself the job of censoring the script of *Porgy and Bess*. The paradox here, of course, is that the thought control usually originates in pressure groups that in all other respects make pious disavowals of literary censorship. The thought control particularly applies in the creation of dialog, so that it is not wildly improbable to guess that the time is not far off when all characters will have to be made to speak according to some censor's idea of cultured expression, and William Faulker's poor whites will be rejudged on the ground that his dialog is somehow insulting to the Negro. The only people on this continent that authors will be able to record will be the Canadians, who are much too touchy already. Luckily I am not going to be around when that happens.

After dialog, the next most obvious example of the kind of thing I study in other novelists is the significant detail. And before I go into that I must remind you that you came here tonight to hear me, and not someone else, so the things I say are me speaking and not Hemingway or Steinbeck or Cozzens or anyone else. Above all they are not the comments of a literary critic of the Marxist persuasion or of organized religion, or of the Columbia boys or the Kenyon crowd. The personal note is not unavoidable, but I am not *trying* to avoid it. In this and the succeeding lecture you will be given what I have to offer, and it is up to you to reject or accept it. I make these statements now because the critics who reluctantly concede that I write good dialog are also the critics who for ten years have been complaining about the detail in my novels. I am slowly winning that little fight. I can't help noticing that little by little, but more and more, the use of detail by newer writers causes the critics to be reminded of the same thing in my novels, and while I don't always gain by this association, at least I am getting my point across, which is that the significant detail really does have significance.

In 1930, three years before I began work on my first novel, I wrote a short story in which no human being appeared. I described in detail, significant detail, the contents of a hotel room. The story was about a thousand words long, which is not long for a short story, so the details had to be the right ones. When you finish reading the story you know that the man who had been occupying the room had been on the town the night before, that he had quarreled with his girl, and that he had committed suicide by jumping out the window. The story was, of course, experimental and a literary tour de force. It was almost bought by a magazine, and the reason it was not bought is macabre in itself: on the day I submitted the story a member of the magazine staff committed suicide by jumping out the window. Now I have just given you a beautiful example of unsignificant detail. The fact that coincidentally a member of the magazine staff committed suicide has no place in this lecture, although it has a certain amount of interest of itself. Significant detail does not at all mean that you take one or two items—a silver cup, say, and an old riding crop—and try to get your effect with the minimum of detail. Sometimes it is desirable to do so. The famous cuff links made of human teeth in *The Great Gatsby* come quickly to mind, and you can supply your own favorite examples of the single significant detail out of your own reading. But the complaint against me in recent years is that I supply too many details. It is not a valid complaint. Many times I have described the contents of a room, or the bric-a-brac on a mantel, and the hasty reader misses the significance of the items I have mentioned. Fortunately I don't give a damn for the hasty reader; if he pays $5 for one of my novels and he wants to throw his money away by skipping or skipping over, that's his loss and not mine. I have done an honest, complete job. If he only wants to listen to the trombones, it's all right with me. I know the violas and cellos are there. I put them there. But detail has to be handled with care, even when the detail is there in abundance. For instance when you are describing a man's clothes you must get everything right, especially the wrong thing. The Junior League girl with her elegant aversion to the objective case was a good example of what I mean. In her case it was a detail of dialog. The same kind of solecism can be demonstrated in a description of a man's clothes. I once described a man who was perfectly dressed except for one small item. He was wearing a double-breasted suit from a good tailor, which meant that it was well cut and fitted him nicely, the material was quiet but distinctive, his shoes came from London and were just right, his necktie was a small-figured one, his shirt was a quiet stripe, from a London shirtmaker. The man was beautifully turned out except for one thing: in his collar instead of a gold safety pin he was wearing a miniature hunting horn. That one detail was significant among all the others and made all the others significant as well. Here was a man with plenty of money, who got his clothes at the best places in New York and London and in all respects but one his taste was correct. But the miniature hunting horn itself was all right; it indicated that he was probably a fox-hunting man or he would not have owned such a pin. The significance was in his wearing the pin with the wrong outfit, and that fact cast doubt over the soundness of his taste. The genuine fox-hunting man would not have worn that pin anywhere but in the field, and certainly not in an outfit that was so carefully and expensively chosen for town wear. The guy, in other words, was a bit of a phony. He could not resist that one vulgarity, and because he could not resist it, he inadvertently proclaimed his dubious standing. The significance of the detail was that everything else was perfection.

Now that kind of detail might not seem important to a great many readers, to most readers, but it was important to me, and because it was important to me, important enough to state it, it could become important to a reader who would ask himself why this author had bothered to include it. My novels are full of such items that I know full well are overlooked by readers, professional and other-wise.

Not longer than a week ago I heard it said over the air that a psychiatrist could tell a lot about you by what kind of car you drove. Well, it's nice to have the head-shrinkers catch up with us, no matter how long they take to do it. Novelists have known for forty years that you could do that. Sinclair Lewis was very good at that. In his day the Buick was as much a badge of your social and economic standing as a Rotary Club button, as the Shriner's ring, as the Elks tooth; and just to make sure that you got the point, Sinclair Lewis would mention the car and the in-signia. But if he had wanted to make a subtler distinction, he could have used the Franklin as a characterizer. To most of you the Franklin is not even a memory, but there was a time when it was as effective for the novelist's purpose as the Buick. In the twenties if you said a man owned a Franklin you would not be talking about the kind of man who owned a Buick, although some Buicks cost the same amount of money as some Franklins. The Franklin-owner would not be wearing an Elks tooth nor a Rotary Club button. He might wear a Masonic pin, but not a Shriner's. The Franklin-owner was more likely to be a tennis player than a golfer, a doctor than a real estate agent, a college man than a noncollege man, and a much more independent thinker than the Buick owner. He would also be likely to own more securities than the Buick owner, whose money would be tied up in personal enterprises. Now why is all this so important to the novelist? It is important because character is so important; it would be out of character for a Buick type man to own a Franklin; it would not be quite so much out of character for a Franklin man to own a Buick. In any case, the novelist has told the reader that Jones owns a Franklin, therefore Jones will behave as a Franklin-owning Jones will behave. And if he behaves in a way that is out of character, either the novelist has been wrong in providing him with a Franklin, or he, the novelist, must explain and make credible the acts that are not in character for the Franklin-owning Jones.

The soundness of the novelist's use of the automobile as a characterizer is not, I think, open to question. It is accepted. But when I was in my teens there was a rather dramatic proof of it in my hometown. It was so long ago that I hope I can be specific without going to prison. In my town there was a man who had a prosperous business. It was a monopoly, in fact. The business was a laundry, and Mr. Sizing, as I shall call him, worked very hard six days a week. He owned a comfortable house on the best street in town. He was married, and he had a son. For six days a week he was always at the laundry, and he and his wife never went out socially. On the seventh day, however, Mr. Sizing would drive his car to a roadhouse which was conducted by the leading madam of our part of the country, and he would spend all day Sunday at the roadhouse. We kids, as well as our elders, always knew when Mr. Sizing was at the roadhouse because we had to pass the roadhouse on our way to the country club. There, every Sunday, when we drove to the club, and still there after we had played golf and had had Sunday night supper, was Mr. Sizing's car. The car was a handsome yellow Stutz Bearcat.

It was completely out of character for a hard-working businessman to own a Stutz Bearcat. But it was not out of character for a man who spent every Sunday at a roadhouse that was conducted by the leading madam. The fascinating part of it all for me, who was already determined to be a writer, was that Mr. Sizing was in appearance more like a man who would spend his time in a roadhouse than he was the hard-working businessman. So I learned as early as that that the significant detail was not merely an arbitrary rule of composition that had been created by the academicians. As an author I have been fascinated by a detail that my wife reported to me last week. She saw a station wagon being driven by a young nun. The little nun was driving along with her arm out the window and her hand resting on the roof. From that one detail I could almost construct a short story, and it would certainly be very helpful in a novel.

A while back I mentioned the hypnotic effect of type, and this seems to be as good a time as any to dwell on that topic. I have discussed dialog and detail, somewhat sketchily, to be sure, but there is a book that I have no intention of writing that would concern itself solely with dialog, and it could be followed by another book, likewise not on my schedule, about detail, and both dialog and detail are related to what I call the hypnotic effect of type, or what might also be called the use of type in mesmerizing the reader.

First let me say that I have never been tempted to

imitate John Dos Passos or E. E. Cummings in their tricks
with type. I am growing more conservative by the hour in
almost everything, but even when I was not at all conservative in my politics and considered myself rather avant
garde in my writing, I did not have to struggle to resist the
temptation to empty the hellbox on a piece of manuscript
paper. I felt then and I believe now that Dos Passos was
making a big mistake, that he was good enough not to
need those tricks, and that the novel form itself still offered plenty of opportunity for experimentation that did
not rely on mechanical devices. I have always used italics
in dialog more than most authors do, for the reason that a
composer uses shaded and unshaded notes. But it is
impossible to do more than an approximation of the
rhythms and tones of speech, and even as I use italics in
dialog I am admitting defeat. If you try to write phonetically you are in danger of writing phony, as do the people
who think they are being naturalistic when they spell
you, y e w. In my never-to-be-written book on dialog I
would make the point that in dialog you could spell the
second person pronoun that way, y e w. But only if the
speaker came from New Jersey, Maryland, Eastern
Pennsylvania, Central Ohio, and certain other parts of the
country where you is not pronounced *yoo* but is pronounced *yew*. Perfect naturalistic representation is impossible of attainment and to attempt it in a novel or short
story is not only to waste your time but also to risk the loss
of the ideal reader's attention. If you doubt me, and if you
have a good enough ear to make the experiment, try to
write a line of dialog phonetically as it would be spoken
by an upper-class Englishman. There simply is no way to
put down the upper-class Englishman's enunciation of
the full vowel sounds. The reason, of course, is that the
Old Etonian does not employ the full vowel sounds.
When he says "how do you do" he says neither *how* nor *do*
nor *you* nor *do*. What's more he probably doesn't give a

damn how you do. And regional sounds in this country can at best only be indicated, the classic example, of course, being the Virginian's four-syllable pronunciation of the word mule. Even I, with my built-in Pennsylvania twang, cannot reproduce in speech or writing the Philadelphian's way of saying "downtown Philadelphia."

So I keep my readily recognizable tricks with type down to the barest minimum. However, I know the potentialities of type, and I am about to demonstrate to you the ill-known fact that the writing of a novel is far from being all there is to the creation of it. The creation and production of a novel has what might be called its own logistics, and I'll go into that later, but first this matter of type. I know type fairly well. When I first went to work as a reporter I was lucky enough to be employed on a scab paper and therefore that ominous rule, don't touch type, was not invoked when I was in the composing room. Thirty years ago I could actually set type and operate, although badly, a linotype machine. I could probably pick it up again in a couple of years, and for the benefit of anyone here who knows anything about type, when I was a kid reporter the compositors on the opposition paper used to throw space-bands at us when we passed their office. It was amusing to us because space-bands cost, I believe, 50 cents apiece, and we were delighted to see that paper going broke. P.S.: It didn't go broke; it took over our paper, but that's another unsignificant detail. Be that as it may, I have always had a love of type and therefore probably was more conscious of it than authors who had never worked around it. I have been a copyreader, which, for the enlightenment of most of you, means I wrote headlines and had to know type. I even did advertising layouts. Consequently when I first read Ernest Hemingway's *A Farewell to Arms* I was so impressed by his paragraphing that I remembered it photographically, and then when I read *The Autobiography of Alice B. Toklas* I realized that in at least one respect the people who said that Gertrude Stein had been an influence on Hemingway were quite correct. My theory was that a reader who did not read English, who looked at the Caporetto retreat passages in *A Farewell to Arms* and at many pages of the Alice B. Toklas book, would be led to believe that both books had been written by the same person. Both books were, of course, published before I wrote my first novel, and while I do not now recall that I made any use of the Hemingway-Stein technique in *Appointment in Samarra*, I am free to admit that beginning with *A Rage to Live*, which I published in 1949, and which I regard as the first novel I wrote in which technique was more than merely construction, I was quite conscious of the effectiveness of that particular Hemingway-Stein technique. I refer especially to the use of great blocks of type that are much too long to be called paragraphs. And here let me say that this technique has no relation to the sentences and paragraphs of William Faulkner, which are another matter entirely. Hemingway, and others before him, including Washington Irving and Sinclair Lewis, instinctively or by design, presented the reader with massive blocks of type that by their massiveness prepare the reader for a great collection of facts even before the reader has had a chance to read the words and sentences. This is a splendid device. For several hundred years the spoken word in novels has had all the typographical breaks, by reason of the fact that said-he and said-she are kept separate and thus subtly the reader is directed to break his attention from he to she, which is what the novelist wants him to do. But in descriptive passages, whether they are descriptive of the contents of a room, or of a fistfight, or of a stream of consciousness, most novelists have been timid about risking the long, unbroken block of type. Consequently they paragraphed descriptions that should have been kept intact. For instance, and to invent a case in point, during the Second World War I visited an atoll in the Pacific after it had been secured by our forces in an action that was said to be one of the most destructive, from the standpoint of shellfire, of the war. To me the only way to describe that island and the effect of that shellfire would have been to put it all in one paragraph or block of type, no matter how long it would run. It was the way I saw it, and I know my job well enough to have picked out the significant details, even if there were hundreds of them, ranging from a single marine's boot lying in a ditch to a lone coconut palm tree that had completely escaped the tons of heavy artillery.

Perhaps one of the reasons for the shorter paragraph and the insistence on it by teachers and editors was the belief that the reader must be pampered. I disagree, on several grounds. In the first place, the novelist owes no more to the reader than to concede that the reader is an intelligent person. Having made that concession, the novelist can then proceed to write as well as he knows how, watching every word along the way, and if he is honest and able, he can forget about pampering the reader. If the reader is too lazy or too stupid to stay with a paragraph because it looks long, then I say the hell with him. The only reader worth bothering about is really no bother at all: he is an anonymous person of sufficient intelligence and curiosity to spend a few hours in the company of a book that a man has worked on for several years. If the novelist has not done his job well, the reader can say the hell with him, too.

Thank you.

2 🛥 Logistics of the Novel

In the first of these lectures I told you a few things about dialog, detail, and the use of type; and I mentioned, without defining, the logistics of the novel. The logistics of the novel is my own phrase, and I do not insist that it is graceful or appropriate or likely to find its way into the language of criticism. But it serves a purpose. The word logistics is of French origin and comes from *loger*, to lodge or quarter, or *logis*, meaning quarters or lodgings. To the military man—and I never heard the word logistics before World War II—it means that branch of the military art which embraces the transport, quartering, and supply of troops. My use of the word is a free adaptation and covers all the preparatory work that a novelist must do before he starts actual writing. You might prefer the word spade-work, but spade-work has a rather cemeterial connotation, and I prefer not to think of its burial before my novel has had any life at all. So let's agree on logistics, at least temporarily. And let me remind you once again, as I did previously, that the opinions expressed and the experiences related are all my own, not those of any other novelist.

The making of a novel starts, of course, with an idea. But what is an idea for a novel? What is—and what is not? I believe that the ultimate, greatest novel of all time will be the one that portrays honestly and completely the life of one man for one day. The novel will contain the best of James Joyce, the best of William Faulkner, the best of Sinclair Lewis, the best of Ernest Hemingway, and, naturally, the best of me. The contribution, or the borrowings from Joyce and Faulkner will consist of the perfecting of what Joyce and Faulkner have done in their tremendous efforts to get down in print the workings of the human brain. More than any other living writer Faulkner comes close to achieving the impossible task of putting the human mind on paper, with a minimum of processing. There will always be processing, at least in the novel as we know it. A couple of hundred years from now there will undoubtedly be a device, based on the electroencephalograph, that will have the power to record the workings of a man's mind, but by that time the novel will be as passé as the cuneiform writings of Abyssinia, or last week's *Time*. Indeed, I predict that the novel will be dead or moribund in less than a hundred years. The nasty world of a hundred years from now will have no time for novels and no place for novelists—or for good manners or whiskey or tobacco or horses or cashmere or families or melody or humor. The passing of the novel will be accompanied by no regret on the part of the world citizens of a century hence. But let me quickly return to the present and as much of the future as belongs to the present, and to a world in which a few men and women care to hear what a novelist has to say about the novel and its creators. This perfect novel, then, will be written by a novelist who can do what Joyce and Faulkner have done and do it more coherently. He will possess the sharp eye that Sinclair Lewis had and a portion of his ironic humor. He will write as lucidly as Ernest Hemingway. And from me—although not really *from* me so much as *like* me—he will have compassion and vitality and a love of truth. It doesn't really matter what man or what kind of man he chooses as the subject of his novel. An author with the equipment I have described would spend the second half of his life in the writing of his novel—the first half having been devoted to the learning of his trade, the mastery of his gifts, the selection of his subject. He would write his novel and then he would do well to change his name and retire to a leprosarium, living out the remainder of his days in good works and contentment, far removed from the outraged many and the the understanding few.

But since that novel has not been written, and that novelist in all probablity has not been born, we here this evening can occupy ourselves with the imperfect novels and highly talented novelists that we know about. I have never discussed this idea with another novelist, this idea

of a single day in the life of one man. But as a matter of fact
I have seldom discussed any idea, his or mine, with
another novelist, at least not in conversation. I have had
correspondence with most of the good ones, and such
correspondence is always stimulating to me and, I hope,
to the others. But novelists of the first rank that are friends
of mine, and with whom I have social relations, are on
holiday when we meet, and so am I. When I was in my
twenties, and before I had written my first novel, I used to
eat and drink with other young writers and our conversations were almost entirely about writing. As I grew older,
and as they did, we wrote our writing and we talked
sport, gossip, politics, painting, music, but rarely literature except when there was a new book by someone
neither of us knew. Oh, there was likely to be a quick
exchange of routine compliments, but no more than that.
The reason was not suspicion or distrust. It was simply
the realization that the less you say about work in progress, the more steam you retain. And when the friendship
is close, the routine compliments mean more than the
gushing of a stranger. Also, to be sure, the routine compliments come in handy when you happen not to have
liked your friend's last book. I supply this information
now because I have never, not once, discussed with
another novelist the more or less abstract question: what
is an idea for a novel? And what is not?

The idea that I have suggested for the perfect novel by a
mythical novelist is, as an idea, so simple that it has often
been used as a short story and even oftener, I suppose, as
part of a novel. That being the case, you might say that
any idea for a novel would also serve as an idea for a short
story; but you would be wrong. An idea for a short story
can be expanded into a full-length novel, but it has been
my experience that when I get an idea for a novel, I see it
almost immediately in terms of the novel, and to try to
squeeze it into the limits of a short story would be to

smother it. I do not want to go into the relative artistic merits of the novel and the short story. There are plenty of little jewels of short stories, and plenty of lumps of peat of novels. But upon recognizing an idea as an idea for a novel, I automatically think of it in no other terms. An idea for a novel comes to me, and keeps coming back to me, with the novel treatment already indicated. How to work out the treatment is another problem, or many other problems, but in general I start with a man, a man that I know a lot about, as I do about hundreds and even thousands of people. It is really amazing how many people I know and how much I know about them, and obviously the explanation for that phenomenon is that I have a good memory. Now when you consider how many people for whom I have my private, unwritten dossiers, it is curious how I happen to reject so many thousands of people, or ignore them, not reject them, and yet accept at a given time a given man as the subject, or idea, for my novel. The subjects, or ideas, for my novel keep coming back insistently and persistently until I actually start work on the book. It is not so much the individual, particular man as he is known to the public, but rather as he is known to me, which may be a very, very different thing from the public knowledge of him. Now begins the very early logistics of a novel.

As I have said in numerous interviews and on the few occasions when I have spoken in public, I do not write what is called the *roman à clef*. But I unhesitatingly use the psychological patterns of real people, as I know them, in creating characters for my novels. My first novel, *Appointment in Samarra*, was apparently about a young man in the country club set of a small Pennsylvania city—the son of a leading physician, product of a good college, attractive, warm, impulsive, and doomed. Inevitably when the novel came out a lot of damn fools tried to identify the character, as damn fools always will. And as

is usually the case with damn fools, they are wrong. They
were almost deliberately, and certainly stupidly, wrong.
The living men that they decided I was writing about had
not, and have not, committed suicide. But because of the
superficial things—the social and economic standing, the
college, the clothes, the drinking habits and so on—
the damn fools picked two friends of mine as the men I
had written about, and the biggest damn fools picked a
third—me. Actually I had created the character Julian
English after contemplating the life and death of a real
person. I used his psychological pattern, and the novel
became what the music people call a standard because I
had been faithful to that pattern. He had been a man of
native intelligence and charm, but he was from the wrong
side of the tracks. I dressed him up, so to speak, in Brooks
Brothers clothes and made him a member of the country
club set, superficialities that were quite sufficient for
superficial readers. When the chips were down, in real
life, my guy committed suicide, which was part of the
psychological pattern and was not only sound but essential. Twenty-five years after the novel was first published
it is still an active property, as they say in Hollywood. This
year, in fact, three studios approached me for the purpose
of buying the screen rights, as though it were a brand new
novel from the Spring list. And those people are no fools,
especially nowadays. When I first went to Hollywood, in
1934, the place was full of cousins and cousins-in-law, but
the pleasant luxury of nepotism is one they no longer can
afford. And quite incidentally, and this is something I
have not seen commented on, one reason why the movies
can afford to pay such high prices for novels and plays is
that there no longer are so many 50 and $100,000-a-year
cousins to be paid. Think of that when you read about the
literary properties that bring three or $400,000. The
cousins and nephews, who not only contributed nothing
but frequently loused things up, have gone, God knows

where and I don't care, and the money that was paid them now goes toward the purchase of the most valuable asset a studio can have, the story. The men who run nearly all the studios today are still businessmen running a business, make no mistake about that, and when they buy a novel or a play they know what they are doing. Nowadays when they buy a novel or a play it goes into production within a year, instead of lying forgotten for years or maybe forever, as used to be the case. As a matter of fact, they started the production preliminaries on a recent novel of mine before the contract had actually been signed, which is, among other things, a measure of mutual good faith. I did not come here to talk about Hollywood, but the motion picture industry buys or tries to buy everything that is good by the best writers in the world, and they are less influenced by personal considerations than the literary cliques and special-interest claques that abound in New York City and Westport, Connecticut, and Rockland County and the halls of ivy.

But to return, after this slight animadversion, to the novel, the idea for the novel, and the *roman à clef*. The use of the psychological pattern of a real person is not a short cut to the creation of characters. It can be very dangerous, and far from being a short cut, it entails a lot of work, more work, possibly, than is involved in the creation of a character out of, as they say, whole cloth—a metaphor that I only vaguely understand. This method, which I have employed successfully in at least four cases, requires a study and knowledge of the real person that is as comprehensive as you would need for a full-scale biography. That explains why I have spent as much as twenty years in contemplation of a character before I start to write about him or her. I will give two examples. The principal character in *A Rage to Live* is a woman called Grace Caldwell. She is based on my study of not one but two women, one of whom was old enough to be the mother of the other. I used the first woman as the basic psychological pattern, and disguised her with the superficial characteristics of the second. But the fascinating thing here was that even as I was writing the novel, the second woman became more and more like the first, so that she actually conformed to the character I had invented, Grace Caldwell. There was a case where life was mirroring art while the art was in the process of creation. That was a very satisfactory confirmation of the authenticity of my character, since the second woman had no way of knowing that she was in my thoughts as I wrote. And incidentally, no one in the world ever guessed correctly the identity of either of the two real women I had in mind while writing *A Rage to Live*, although there were dozens of guesses.

The second example I give you had to do with a later novel of mine, *Ten North Frederick*, of which the principal character is Joe Chapin. In that instance I took a real person whose life was rather dramatically changed by an episode that made a tremendous difference in his mode of living. The episode occurred when my real life person was a grown man, and a man set in his ways. Now what I, the novelist, did was to pretend that the dramatic episode— over which, by the way, he had no control—had never occurred. What kind of man would this be, how would he have turned out, if the episode had not occurred? From then on I wrote pure fiction. I became what Thornton Wilder calls the god-novelist, the novelist who has the power of life and death over all his creatures.

I promised you two examples. Now I can't resist giving you a third. It concerns the character Alfred Eaton, whose story I tell in *From the Terrace*. Here again I used a real-life psychological pattern, which involved a great deal of study, especially since the real person is not an American and I have never met him. But everything that has happened to the man, and also to his first wife, since I first began to write that novel, has fitted in with my analysis of him and of her, and with the implied prognosis that is the ending of *From the Terrace*.

I have written only one *roman à clef*, which was my second novel, *Butterfield 8*. It is hardly any secret that I based that novel on the story of Starr Faithfull, the tragic young woman of the 1930s whose tragedy seems to have been repeated in 1959. One of the things that pleased me most about that novel was that a year ago, twenty-three years after *Butterfield 8* was published, a distinguished historian whose name you would all recognize, told me that *Butterfield 8* would be indispensable to any historian who attempted to write about the twentieth century in the United States. Then on second thought he added *Appointment in Samarra*, and made the shocking admission that those were the only books of mine he had read. I find it in my heart to forgive him because his work has been concerned with the eighteenth and nineteenth centuries, and I am very pleased that he ever got around to me at all.

He raised, and I now re-raise, a point that I would like to comment on and that was once offered to me as the topic of a lecture. The topic was: The Novelist as Social Historian.

I don't know why we novelists feel so complimented when we are called social historians, but we do. Most social historians are pretty dull writers, and could not be successful novelists. But I suppose we are still suffering from the nineteenth century attitude toward the novel, which was continually denounced from the pulpit as trash. Good novels, fine novels, great novels were being written in the nineteenth century, but the clergy apparently found the time to read only the trashy ones—or, quite possibly, the clergy had no better literary judgment then than the Marxist critics have today. In any event, we novelists are rather pathetically pleased when we see ourselves described as social historians, just as I was pleased by the remarks of the historian I spoke of a moment ago. To my way of thinking, the social history that appears in a novel is of importance if it is that kind of novel, but only of secondary importance. When a novel's social-history content begins to take over, the author is in trouble. If the social history part does not relate to his characters, the author is converting himself into historian or journalist. From Harriet Beecher Stowe to John Steinbeck the author who offers social history is most effective, perhaps even *only* effective, when his concern is for his characters rather than for his conditions. The difference between a novel about sharecroppers and a novel about Ezra Bumpkin, sharecropper, is the difference between a social-history report on the one hand and, on the other, Art. No one knew that better than Edith Wharton, who wrote with understanding and precision about people in New York society, and then with the same understanding and precision created Ethan Frome, which is proof of the verity of Art and an example of the versatility of the artist. The novelist ought to be, must be, on the side of Art. If he writes as a social historian first, I even doubt that his social history will be much good, since his understanding of, let us say, the sharecroppers' conditions is limited by his observations of the general and his remoteness from the particular. Edith Wharton knew it. Sinclair Lewis knew it. But the author who is consciously, or perhaps I should say self-consciously, a social historian is almost certain to be writing from a point of view that has been determined for him; he writes to conform to a social or political or religious doctrine that is not his own. He may love it and may have adopted it, but it was not his invention; it was only his discovery, which is far from the same thing. Consequently, in writing to conform to a social or political or religious doctrine or philosophy, he compels himself to write for the approval of the exponents or practitioners of the doctrines or the philosophies. And that is such a big mistake that mistake is an inadequate

word for it. Artistically, it means the self-destruction of
the author. Every word that an artist, or author—in this
context the words are interchangeable—puts down on
paper should and must be his own, and that cannot be the
case if the author is writing social history from the point of
view of Karl Marx or Thomas Aquinas or Winston Churchill or Elsa Maxwell or H. L. Mencken or Will Rogers or
Roscoe Pound or Ezra Pound—or me. It is a calamity
when a writer writes for the approval of anyone else; it is a
tragedy when a man who writes well fails to learn from
the calamity. A reasonable skill with words is not too
uncommon, but the thing that sets the first-rate apart
from the merely skillful is that combination of talent and
independence of thought and expression that is the first
essential to art. Art, which goes merrily on resisting definition, may be described as an imitation of life. The
imitation is performed by one gifted person, and understood by at least one other person. But an imitation of the
imitation is no longer art, no matter how good it may be as
imitation or of itself.

The novel can be art, the novelist an artist, and we
should be polite but aloof when we are given the well-
intentioned compliment of being called social historians.
Social history has absolutely no standing in the world of
art as I see it. And whether or not you will pardon me for
saying so, my decision as to what is art in the novel is
final. In that respect I have no modesty, and certainly no
humility. The humility that I have, and any artist has, is
actively present while I am writing a novel, and is more
recognizably described as the artistic conscience. It is the
thing that makes you search through five dictionaries for
the right word—and the rejection of the word because it
may not belong in a particular sentence or sequence of
sentences. It is the right phrase in dialog, the significant
detail in description, the decision to use that certain man
or that certain woman as the leading character of a novel.

It is the creation and guided evolution of techniques that I could not possibly go into now but that I can hint at by saying that they come under the two headings of strategy and tactics. And oddly enough, the humility that is activated as artistic conscience keeps the artist from stopping at social history and instead makes him go on to the art of the novel.

It is a pleasure to write a good novel, if you are writing it for yourself as an artist. It is hard work, but hard work is a pleasure if you are your own boss, and sometimes when you are not your own boss but are doing what you like to do. When I read of or hear an author saying that he hates to write, I want to say, "Well, why do it?" Mind you, almost every author I have known, including myself, has found and can still find excuses to dodge work. The temptation is always there when you are your own boss, but I know that the good ones are happiest when they are at work. They may not be at their social best, but who gives a damn about that? For most of us it is at least as much of a chore to make the social effort as it is to do honest, pleasurable, satisfactory if not satisfying work. The writer who finds writing a chore, rather than work, gets no sympathy from me. The late Percy Hammond was once asked to state his idea of fun. "Not writing," he said, and has been quoted a thousand times. But what did Percy Hammond do for a living? He was a drama critic. A graceful, felicitous essayist, the like of whom, except for the also late Wolcott Gibbs, we have not seen since Percy Hammond died. But a drama critic in one season sits in judgment on fifty to a hundred plays, all the work of other men, the extended, good, bad, or indifferent work of other men. Subconsciously at least, fifty to a hundred times a season he is reminded of what he has not done himself, and in such circumstances writing *could not* be fun. In what I am sure will be a passing mood of tolerance, I may say that the wonder is that the regular reviewers of plays and books are any good at all. Of course there are all told only about a dozen critics in the entire United States who are worth taking seriously, so my mood of tolerance has not been so costly.

At the mention of fun in connection with the work of writing we respond immediately by association of the word fun with the word writing, leaving out that other word, work. And here we get on a subject that I talk about every time I speak in public and a great many times when I am talking in private. Some years ago I read a paper at the Elizabethan Club at Yale which I consider the most successful paper I ever read. The Elizabethan Club is an organization of students and faculty and alumni who have an interest in literature. I spoke to a packed house, and what I said could not have been wholly acceptable to all present that night, and yet I regard my lecture as successful because so far as I know, no one who was present on the occasion has become a novelist or play-wright. My argument was intended to discourage young men who were thinking of becoming writers. I will al-ways discourage anyone who is thinking of becoming a writer. If by the time a man is a sophomore in college he has not passed the point of indecision, he should be discouraged. The title of my Elizabethan Club paper was "The Rewards of Writing," and twelve years after I made my points I feel even more strongly that I am performing an act of kindness when I redirect, or try to redirect, those who are thinking of becoming writers. You do not think of becoming a writer; you *know* that you are a writer, with even fewer doubts, I suspect, than the doubts that bother a young man who suspects that he should study for the priesthood. You can have doubts as to the attractiveness or desirability of becoming a banker, a broker, a certified public accountant, a pickpocket, a spy, a politician, or the manager of a miniature golf course, to name a few occupa-tions that a high school senior may consider. Time and circumstances may take care of the future of this not so mythical high school senior, and the boy who is disposed to become a pickpocket may end up as a politician. The one who would like to manage a miniature golf course could very easily find happiness and profit as a broker. But when a young man tells me he is thinking of becoming a writer I have an evil suspicion that I am listening to a potential bum.

Yale is a rich university, attended by many young men from rich families, but it seemed to me just as important to discourage the rich from becoming bums as to give counsel to boys whose families could less well afford the extremely unwholesome sight of a time-wasting, money-wasting no-talent Joe. It wasn't so much that I cared what happened to the sons of the rich, although some of my best friends have money; but I care a great deal about the standing of writing in the national community, and I would like to see the no-talent bums pretend they are doing something else. The writing occupation is too often used as an excuse for doing nothing and for doing it with a great deal of insolence and arrogance. Writing is work. Work is honorable. I don't want writing *or* work dishonored by young men who lie to themselves and to their families. I don't want the writing occupation to be a catch-all for lazy, untalented, dishonest people. I don't want the profession I love, the work I love, to attract people who see it as a justification for getting drunk, leading irregular hours, rejecting the conventions—and doing nothing. That is what I meant by the association of the word fun with the word writing. All through the centuries that man has had reading and writing, and particularly creative writing and pleasurable reading, there have been writers who drank too much, who slept where and when they felt like it, and who rebelled at the social restrictions of their times. But I firmly believe, as a man who had a coast-to-coast reputation for workouts with the bottle, that no one ever wrote anything good while stewed. I never wrote anything worth printing when I had even a slight glow, although I hastily concede that the amount that it took me to induce a slight glow would have put some people in the drunk tank. True, I have seen a man write a newspaper column between nips from a flask, and they were readable, entertaining columns; but I am talking about creative writing here; novels, short stories, plays. And of course I am not talking about poetry or poets. I consider myself an authority on poets, as a result of vast experience, but I know nothing about poetry. On the other hand I not only know a great deal about the novel and the short story, I also am well acquainted with the men and women who write them. They work. But they are not seen at work. They are seen when they are relaxing, or escaping from, or dodging work. The novelist who stumbles into "21," the short story writer who bobbles around Costello's—they are not working, but it is what the public sees and has seen for hundreds of years. You may not be able to reach a novelist by telephone when you call him at noon; you are told he is still asleep. But at five-thirty that morning he was working as hard as a man can work, using his brains and using up his physical strength. That, however, is a part of his life that the young man who is thinking of becoming a writer never knows about. One night last year I sat at the typewriter for eight solid hours, and when I decided to call it quits and got up from my desk, my legs buckled under me, and I fell. I would not ask anyone else to work that hard, nor would I subject myself to such treatment if I did not love my work. So you can see that I have some reason to scorn the people who call themselves writers but are in reality pretentious bums.

This is a large class, and there are as many reasons for taking this course as there are students taking it. Each of you has his or her own reason. But I hope none of you enrolled in order to learn how to write a novel. The writing of a novel cannot be taught. You can be taught to write an acceptable newspaper story, to prepare advertising copy, and, I suppose, to write the kind of slop that you are offered on television and in most movies, even today. It seems to me that every few months I see on television a new but not very different version of the autobiographical story of the TV writer who goes to Hollywood and is ruined. Ruined? What was there to ruin? Aside from the movie *Marty* I can't think of anything that was done by a television writer that I consider first-rate, and bear in mind that it was the *movie Marty* and not anything that the author did on television that I consider first-rate. Last winter I watched a television feature which consisted of half a dozen television writers discussing their work and their medium. To me it was one of the comedy shows of the season, although it was not so intended. These were, by the way, the writers who are television's own big names. I have never met any of these people, a condition which I shall try to make chronic, and so I have no idea how they got their first TV writing jobs or how they achieved their anthill eminence. Although it is easier to understand how they became prominent than to understand how they got their jobs. How they got their jobs is a complete mystery, but my theory to explain their prominence is fairly simple; one word: perseverance. They kept at it; and in a medium where submediocrity is Phi Beta Kappa, three purchased scripts is accomplishment. If the subject matter is juvenile delinquency, for instance, or any other topical item, a script is automatically regarded as documentary, as social history, as sociology; and if the boys and girls wear blue jeans and pony tails and the camera lingers on their blackheads, Jack Gould will call it valid and Jack Crosby will call it frightening, and both will solemnly conclude that TV has once again gained stature or maturity. That kind of writing, supported by that kind of criticism, can be taught. There is no reason why we should not have as many second-story schools teaching that kind of writing as there are Arthur Murray dance studios. I sometime suspect that the reason you hear so many cracks about the movies on TV is that the movies, especially the English movies, such pictures as *Tight Little Island* and my favorite *Scotch on the Rocks*, provide a contrast that is not at all favorable to the originals, so called, on the hour and hour and-a-half dramatic shows. I also suspect that the reason for the submediocrity of the TV dramatic presentations can be found in the pompous ignorance of the TV producers. I am fond of money, but money in such vast quantities, placed at the disposal of the tasteless sharpies who produce TV shows, is an enemy of good writing.

And I am not a literary snob. Well, maybe I am. But let me put it this way: I am more than tolerant of good hack writing. Short stories in the *Saturday Evening Post*, the late *Collier's* and sometimes in the detective story magazines are not bought for literary merit, but oftener than you may realize, hack stuff has had a way of becoming literature. Ring Lardner and F. Scott Fitzgerald are names that come to mind. William Faulkner is of course a frequent *Post* contributor. But I am not thinking of them so much as I am of the good writing by writers who never get highbrow recognition. I can recall that when I was a boy, first reading the Sherlock Holmes stories, I was told they were trash. Now, when I am fifty-four years old and know something about writing, I read those stories over and over again, not because I care about the plots, but because Sir Arthur Conan Doyle created hundreds of credible characters and permanently made available the manners and customs of his time. He was, if you like, a social historian, although he was considered a hack.

Now that kind of writing cannot be taught either. It is professional writing. It is often the hardest kind of writing, in that it is simple, unpretentious, written for entertainment alone and yet done with such expertness and sincerity that the highbrow delightedly or against his will must describe it as literature. And yet when the author has finished with it he cannot enjoy the most satisfactory experience in writing, which is the satisfaction, self-satisfaction, if you like, he has produced a work of art. Mind you, no novel is perfect, any more than any work of art is perfect; but a novel that the author can believe in as a work of the art of the novel, is the most satisfying, inspiring experience in writing. The layman is all wrong about inspiration. Inspiration does not come to the author at the conception of a novel. It comes when the novel has been finished. Good work completed is the most inspiring event in the novelist's professional life—but first he must do the work.

I was in London a few weeks ago and had a press conference with British reporters. One of them asked me to reveal the secret of writing successful novels, and I replied by telling him a story that many of you have heard. A long-haired musician, a foreigner, happened to stop in front of Birdland, where he said to a hipster: "Please, sir, vill you tell me how I get to Carnegie Hall?"

The hipster looked at the longhair and said: "Practice, man, practice."

3 🖋 Method and Technique of the Novel

Since my last appearance at Rider College I have had two birthdays, and I have published a long novel and three novellas. So you see these lectures are profitable to me, no matter what they may be to you. For those of you who are attending these lectures for the first time, perhaps

I ought to explain that I practically never give lectures or do any other kind of public speaking. I am no good at it, which will soon be apparent, and it takes a lot of time out of my heavy work schedule. But Dr. Kent and Dr. Taylor came to me two years ago with a different approach. An approach, I may say, that would not have been available to the people at, for instance, the University of Wisconsin, and even less so for the people at Leland Stanford. When Dr. Kent and Dr. Taylor invited me to speak at Rider, they politely suggested that it would be a neighborly gesture on my part. I could not say no to that neighborly pitch, so here I am for the third time. And probably, I might add, for the last. I was only a kid of fifty-four when I made my other appearances but now I am fifty-six, and the days dwindle down—to a precious few . . .

Still, as I said before, the experience has been profitable to me. Or to put it more precisely, it has not been unprofitable. In my fifties I have become even more of a compulsive author than I was when I was younger, and in this orgy of work since my last visit to Rider I not only have completed a full-length novel and written three novellas; I also compulsively wrote about two dozen short stories, which will be published in a collection next fall, and I compulsively wrote a three-act comedy and two other novellas. I also had to get new glasses. But the greatest pleasure in life for me, or at least the greatest pleasure that I care to speak of in a college lecture—is work. Any time I take away from my work, or that others take away from my work, is given up reluctantly. At the moment I am writing a long novel which I am calling *The Lockwood Concern*. God willing, it should be completed sometime next year, and I shall then go to work on something else. But it probably is a good thing once in a while to stop writing. Go out to recess. Take ten.

Now I could be very pompous with you and say that it does one good to get outside one's work, to view it from a different perspective. Or I could pretend that I had some other scholarly reason for interrupting the creative process. But why kid you, and why kid myself? One of the rewards of advancing age is that you don't have to kid yourself, and indeed, you'd better not. The truth is, the only way I can get any pleasure out of stopping work is to stop writing—and talk about it. And when I say talk about writing, I mean talk about my writing. And so, since that is a subject on which I am uniquely qualified to speak, that's what I am going to do. I trust that you will be as polite as my previous Rider College audiences; I saw only two sound sleepers, and neither of them snored very loud. If I happen to mention other authors in the course of my lecture, be not deceived. I am not here to talk about anybody but myself or anyone else's work but my own.

The aspect of my work that has come in for the greatest discussion in the past year has been the length of it. The varying lengths of various pieces of work. My three novellas, which were published together as a trilogy called *Sermons and Soda-Water*, got quite good reviews. About 80 percent favorable reviews, I guess, which for me is exceptionally high. I have never been called an inspirational author, God knows and thank God, but I do inspire the critics to new heights of scorn and vituperation. There is a woman who reviews for one of the quality magazines who I think is in serious trouble. You cannot hate anyone as much as she admits she hates me, without having met me, unless you are a little off your rocker. You do not subject yourself to the torture of reading four books in a single year by an author who can drive you to such self-revealing statements. There is nothing easier than the act of closing a book. You don't even have to close it; let it fall from your hands and it may even close itself. This miserable women probably sticks pins in herself when there's no book of mine within easy reach. But she belongs in the 20 percent outright unfavorable. Among the 80 percent fa-

vorable there were, I should say, about half who praised
the trilogy, but with a big exception taken. To sum up this
50 percent of 80 percent, they said that the novellas were
fine, and such a relief from my long novels. The word
monster, I regret to say, has been appearing quite frequently. My long novels have also been called marathon
and nonstop. A marathon, by the way, stops at 26 miles,
but we are not here governed by the rules of a track meet,
and book reviewers who use athletic metaphors hardly
ever know what they're talking about.

Now the interesting thing about the critics' concern
with the length of my books, or one of the interesting
things, is this: the reading public, the men and women
who pay five or six dollars for one of my novels, are
supposed to be less patient with an author than the literary boys and girls. The legend is that the literary folk,
being literary folk, are willing to spend more time with a
book than the business or professional men and their
wives and daughters and mothers. But that is simply not
so. My longest novel, *From the Terrace*, has also been, in
the trade edition, the hard-cover six dollar edition, the
biggest seller. In the hard-cover edition I think it sold
about a quarter of a million copies. In the paperback it is
one of the biggest sellers in the world, well up in the
millions, but let's confine ourselves for the moment to the
hard-cover acceptance by the men and women who buy
books, and the attitude of the critics, who don't buy them
but get them free and then resell them.

I am compelled to observe that the critical opposition to
my long books is due to one factor: a critic can read, and
write reviews of, three or four short novels in the same
time he takes to read a *From the Terrace*. It comes down to
that simple fact. A critic who writes, say, three 500-word
reviews a week, is irritated by a *From the Terrace* because
after spending all that time—all *what* time?—reading my

long novel, he has only the material for a single review. It's as simple and as disgusting as that.

Yes, disgusting. Because in among the reviews of my trilogy, the favorable or half-favorable reviews, over and over again I came across a frank warning not to write any more long books. This is no exaggeration. Those of you who read *Sermons and Soda-Water*, the trilogy, will recall that in my foreword I said that I was at work on a *long* novel, that would probably be my longest. Now mind you, this is a novel that will not be completed for another year, no critic in the United States has the faintest idea what the novel is going to be about, or whom it is going to be about; or the locale, or the period in history or anything else about it. But I have been told in so many angry words that I cannot expect it to receive favorable reviews. That is why I use the word disgusting, and for good measure add the word disgraceful. It is disgraceful, because it proves better than anything I might say, the sorry state of American literary criticism.

In all my experience in the theatre world, the movie world, the book world, I have never seen anything like those warnings. Louella Parsons, whom you cannot take seriously, did, back in 1940, try to prevent the production and then the release of the movie *Citizen Kane*, and I seem to recall that Hedda Hopper, whom only Louella Parsons takes seriously, has come out against a movie production of *Lolita*. But these two old women have no influence, and they certainly have no standing in the intellectual community. If Walter Kerr, of the *Herald Tribune*, or Brooks Atkinson of the *Times* or his fumbling successor Mr. Taubman, had issued a warning to a playwright that his next year's play was going to get a bad notice because it was four acts long, the protest would be noisier than Sardi's at lunchtime. Would any music critic dare to announce that he was going to pan Roy Harris's next symphony because it was going to run an hour and ten minutes instead of the usual forty-five? The very idea, of course, is preposterous, but my situation is analagous. I have been told, over and over again, that the novel I am working on is going to be panned because of its length.

The ridiculously ironic touch here is that most of the critics fancy themselves as eggheads, and one of the favorite targets of the egghead is condensation. The eggheads love to kid digests, quick culture, shortcuts to intellectual status. And rightly so. But when it comes to the length of novels, or my novels, to be specific, I am threatened with extinction if I do not conform—note that word—to the 300-page limit.

The length or brevity of any serious literary work has nothing whatever to do with a serious author's treatment of the work, no matter what the critics say. *From the Terrace* was about 900 pages long. Well, I assure you that it could have been a great deal longer; as far as I'm concerned, and I am the only one who could possibly know, there is not a surplus word in that 900-page novel. It took 900 pages to do what I wanted to do, and I always knew, with great accuracy, how long it was going to be. Some of you may have read a slim volume of mine called *A Family Party.* In book form it is 64 pages long. That is all it needed to be, all I ever intended it to be. *Appointment in Samarra* is 301 pages long; it could have been about 30 pages shorter, but it was my first novel. *A Rage to Live* is 590 pages long; it should have been longer and it was, but I allowed myself—for the last time; this was 1949—to be persuaded to cut about 40 pages, a great mistake on my part, because what I cut belonged in the novel. So, for a serious and skillful author—and I claim I am both—the length of a novel, a novella, or a short story is determined by the author's decision as to the method he is going to use in order to say what he wants to say. I do not tailor my stories to suit any commercial publication requirements; I don't have to. Nearly everything I write gets printed, and it gets printed the way I want it or not at all. I have been publishing fiction for more than thirty years, and in that time I have acquired a reputation and with the reputation, a following, so that while my books enjoy varying degrees of success, none of them nowadays is a total flop. If that were not so, I might be inclined to knuckle under if a publisher suggested that I stretch out some manuscripts and cut down some others, although I doubt it. I have always been rather independent, which is the understatement of the evening.

What, you may ask, determines an author's decision as to the method he is going to use, and therefore the length a story will run? Well, if you want to know what determines William Faulkner's decisions, you'll have to ask him. But I'm here, and I'll try to tell you what influences my decisions.

I'm afraid that the truthful answer is not an altogether satisfactory one, but truthfully, the method I use on a given story depends first of all on author's instinct. I don't know whether you're born with it, or you acquire it through years of creative writing, but I do know that somewhere along the line you become aware of it, and if you have enough self-confidence, you learn to trust your instinct. It's almost always right.

Out of somewhere you get an idea for a story. Frequently, at least with me, it is not a story idea but a character idea. This is old stuff to those of you who have heard me before, but I reserve the right to repeat myself and even to contradict myself. That's the kind of lecturer I am. So I get a character idea, and that is often all I need to get started on a story. As I told you in, I think, my second lecture, I get my character placed somewhere and start him talking to someone, and pretty soon the character takes form, for the dialog, if it is true, is self-revealing right away. The dialog establishes the economic-social-

educational status of the character, and very soon establishes the circumstances of the scene in which he is speaking. Before I have finished two pages of manuscript my
author's instinct has told me how much I want to tell
about this character, and thus the length of the story is
dictated by my wish. You understand, of course, that I
employ this method in writing short stories, which vary
in length from 1,500 to 15,000 words, which is quite a
variation. With a novel, however, my method is different.

A novel is a big, big job, and some of you will recall my
speaking of the logistics of the novel. Let me develop that
thought. The decision to write a novel—or not to write
one—is something to be taken very seriously. One of the
first things you must decide is: am I willing to devote a
year or more of my life to the creative and physical effort
that a novel is going to require. When you are in your
fifties, an age when you read the obituary pages as a daily
habit, you are influenced by considerations of creative
and physical effort in terms of time. It comes down to this:
can I afford to spend a year of my life in the writing of this
novel? Do I feel that these people, the principal characters
in my novel, are going to hold as much fascination for me
six months from now as they do today? To put it another
way, am I going to want to live with them six months from
now? For I assure you, they do live with you and you with
them, and if they are not interesting company—not
necessarily attractive, but interesting—you may find that
you have wasted seven or eight months of your creative
effort and seven or eight months of your life. Thus it
actually becomes a life and death decision, although that
may seem to be an overdramatization.

Now in my case another thing I have to decide before I
make a novel out of this person or these people, is, how
special are these characters? I deny that I am a social
historian; I am a novelist, and a social historian only
incidentally. Nevertheless my novels do partake of the

elements and classification of social history, and behind
my decision to make a novel is the question, can I say
what I want to say about my times as well as what I want
to say about my people, my characters? I would never be
guilty of the self-conscious, awkward cut-outs that Mr.
Dos Passos passes off as documentary novels. I will not
resort to typographical tricks either. But I most certainly
want to tell about my times without going in for decou-
page. The novelists, as distinguished from the stylists, that
I most admire, have all done what I want to do and have
done. Dickens, Howells, Doyle, Tarkington, Galsworthy,
Lewis, Fitzgerald, they all caught and put down the circumstances of their times, and I do it too, and the more
proficient I become, the more I am likely to make my
comments on my times. I have done it from the beginning
of my career, with *Appointment in Samarra*, which is a live
novel twenty-seven years after first publication. I did it
with *Butterfield 8*, which twenty-six years after publication sold a million copies in one year in the paperback
edition. The sale was helped, of course, by the movie
production, but it would not have sold a million in one
year—and still selling—if the novel itself had not been
readable. Nor do I believe that the rather tame sex in the
novel, judged by 1961 standards, is wholly responsible for
the sale. I am not knocking sex, nor am I apologizing for
its presence in my novels; I think the many millions who
read books are just a little more sophisticated about sex
than the egghead critics or the clergy give them credit for.
I know from my mail that the nonprofessional public are
neither as pruriently sex-conscious nor as hypocritically
alarmed as the critics on *Time* or *Newsweek* or other more
or less egghead publications.

But I digress, as I fully intend to do when I feel like it. I
was saying that I carefully consider, before deciding to
write a novel, what opportunities a story offers for my
comments on my times. And I guess I didn't digress very

much when I discussed sex. *Butterfield 8* told a story of the early thirties, and nobody could deny that it was a true one, since it was based on a real-life tragedy of the time. A lot of people didn't like the book, but then there are a lot of people that I don't like, too.

But to proceed: there is a third consideration of great importance to me when I am making up my mind as to how I am going to present a story. This third consideration is a more subtle one than the possibility of my losing interest in my characters, and also more subtle than the social comments I may want to make. It is, this third consideration, the technique consideration. Every novel I write is technically different from all the other novels I have written. Some of these differences are, of course, readily apparent. You do not need an M.A. in American Lit to detect the technical differences between *Ourselves to Know* and *Hope of Heaven*, or the technical differences between the novellas of *Sermons and Soda-Water* and the novel *Ten North Frederick*. *Ourselves to Know*, which gave the giant intellect on the *Trenton Sunday Advertiser* a bad time, is already a best seller in England, was a best seller in this country, and is now on its merry way to success in the paperbacks, all of which, as usual, will be explained away by the critics as positive proof that the United States and the United Kingdom are populated by people who have nothing better to do than bury their dirty noses in dirty books. Actually, however, the egghead critics were so busy burying their dirty noses in the sex passages of *Ourselves to Know* that they generally overlooked the technique of the novel. If all I had wanted to do was to write a dirty book, I certainly blew the opportunity there. I have never written a dirty book, I have never written an immoral book. I have never even written an amoral book. I was once asked to write a dirty book. A very rich man, a now retired international banker who is one of the eggiest eggheads in the country, invited me to prepare a tidbit for his private collection. I laughed in his silly face. As to *Ourselves to Know*, a highly respected monsignor of the Roman Catholic faith recently told my mother that I am his favorite novelist, that *Ourselves to Know* is his favorite novel of mine, and that not even a theologian could have written the scene in the prison more accurately than I wrote it. But you wouldn't have got that impression from the *Trenton Sunday Advertiser*. I daresay the local boy considers himself a more competent judge of a moral book than a Catholic monsignor, and I think that comment just about takes care of him. The fact is that very few critics discussed the theological aspects of that novel, as few as those who gave much thought to the technical aspects. They were preoccupied with the sex passages, possibly because they are overimpressed by Graham Greene. But for the serious critics of the novel there were in *Ourselves to Know* as in all my novels, points of technique that eluded them or that they had no time for before rushing to the next attack. In a recent TV discussion one well-known author—not a critic, an author—stated that my work will outlive the work of the various other prominent novelists under discussion. If that is so, the time will come when more attention is paid to the details of technique that are there for any present-day critic to see, if he knows how to look for them. Fortunately, I haven't got the time or the desire to indicate or explain them now, but I assure you that they are there. I have the grey hairs to prove it.

The thing about technique that I do want to say a few words about this evening is that at fifty-six, and after all those millions of words, I am still learning. If I went on writing one novel after another without innovating in every one, I would be so bored that I would quit writing novels and write only for Hollywood. The government takes away nearly all of the money I earn, so the principal compensation I get out of my work is in the work itself, when I am satisfied with it or when I have learned something from it. I'm sure I have made well over a million dollars, but you don't have to take a course in accounting to guess how much I was permitted to keep from the benevolent gentlemen in Washington. And what I was allowed to keep, I did not keep very long or much of. So when a critic or a layman suggests that I write for money, he is only revealing himself as an economic blockhead or a tax dodger. I have made, through my work, quite a few million dollars for other people—publishers, actors, directors, musicians, critics—but I must confess that my pleasure in that accomplishment is no greater than their gratitude to me, and you can put that under your contact lens without fear of irritation. You must have some incentive to work as hard as I do, and you may call it dedication, but it is still incentive. Whatever you call it, it must come from within yourself, as pride emanates from something within yourself, your egotism and your egotistical apprehensions; self-confidence gained from an honest self-appraisal of your control of your craftsmanship, and the lack of self-confidence that at some time or other plagues every artist in every form of art. I came across a provocative statement by Joseph Conrad the other night. Oddly enough Conrad makes the statement in the Author's Note to his novel *Victory*, and I quote: "Thinking," says Joseph Conrad, "is the great enemy of perfection."

That sounds rather more like Oscar Wilde than Joseph Conrad. "Thinking is the great enemy of perfection." I was slightly tempted to send that statement to my friend Robert Oppenheimer at the Institute for Advanced Study, but I'm sure the people at the Institute would easily dispose of Conrad's aphorism. One way to dispose of it, of course, would be not to think about it. In fact, that would be the perfect way, would it not? But let us consider Conrad's statement in its context. He is talking about his character Axel Heyst, and he says: "Heyst in his fine detachment had lost the power of asserting himself. I don't mean the courage of self-assertion, either moral or physical, but the mere way of it, the trick of the thing, the readiness of mind and the turn of the hand that come without reflection and lead the man to excellence in life, in art, in crime, in virtue and for the matter of that, even in love. Thinking is the great enemy of perfection. The habit of profound reflection, I am compelled to say, is the most pernicious of all the habits formed by the civilized man." End of quotation.

Now I, in my simple, uncomplicated way, do not go along with Joseph Conrad. But I see what he means when he speaks of the readiness of mind and the turn of the hand that come without reflection and lead the man to excellence in life and in art. I not only see what he means; I have said something similar when I declared that my author's instinct tells me how much I want to tell about a character, and thus determine the length of a story. But if I accepted Conrad's statement I would have to rely wholly on my creative instinct, and I am not sure that I would even want to do that. I think William Faulkner does it—not entirely, but more consistently than any other author. Curiously enough, Dos Passos, who is the author Faulkner most admires among his contemporaries, does just the opposite; he thinks so much that he forgets the novelist's first duty, which is the creation of character. When I have read Dos Passos I always feel that I am in the presence of a man with a pair of scissors and a glue pot, going through a copy of the *New York Times* and stopping every once in a while to say, "Ah, here's a good one." I have never felt that I was in the presence of an artist or of a creative force. On the other hand, while reading Faulkner I have always felt that I was in the presence of an artist, of a creative force, even though the art and the creative force get to be too much for me. Faulkner, I have often said, is a genius, the only one in our time that I know about, and for those of you who have not heard me say it, I shall add my reason for saying it: William Faulkner is the one author among us all who comes closest to putting it down on paper, from thought to printed word, with the least processing in between. That explains why he seems incoherent. But Faulkner is unique, and I would not be Faulkner if I could be. I get pleasure out of working, and I am almost sure Faulkner does not. As I said before, every time I start work on a new novel I set myself problems in technique. The most overworked word in the language at the moment is challenge. It pops up in just about every political speech, and in discussions of all sorts, and in the commercials on radio and TV. It is as overworked as those recent favorites, valid and validity, and has become meaningless. Nevertheless I'm afraid I'm going to have to use it, because it belongs here, properly: the technical problems I set up for myself are challenges, my artist conscience challenging my craftsmanship. I stack the deck, naturally. I do not set up impossible obstacles of technique; but believe me I do not make it easy for myself, and the fact that I make mistakes and am not always altogether successful is all the proof I need that I play fair. It is also, of course, very gratifying when I am successful, and incidentally I do not consider that I have been successful when I just squeak through. Perhaps thinking *is* is the great enemy of perfection, maybe Conrad is right. But I have a little secret for you: the perfect novel will never be written. Obviously it is not going to be written by a man who enjoys working as much as I do.

Since this is to be my final lecture at Rider College, and since I am an old valdeictorian—Niagara Prep, 1924, a school that ceased to exist that same year—my concluding remarks should be of a valedictory nature. Literally, of course, a valedictory is only a farewell; but through the years the word has taken on other meanings, so that a valedictorian is expected to speak with all the wisdom he has acquired thus far, preempting some of the functions of the salutatorian and the class historian and class poet and the baccalaureate preacher. Well, I have already told you that I agreed to give these lectures because the invitation was put to me on a basis of neighborliness. That, however, was not the only pitch that Drs. Taylor and Kent made. They also told me that I would be the first novelist to lecture under the new liberal arts degree curriculum. I have a sense of history, and I am not at all sure that that distinction did not appeal to me more than the mere geographical one of neighborliness. I may not be the best visiting lecturer under the liberal arts program, but by God I was the first, and when Rider celebrates its centennial as a liberal arts college, late in the twenty-first century, I trust that some mention will be made of me. I shall not threaten to haunt those twenty-first-century ceremonies; I have no desire to live in those times, even as a ghost. But I would like to think now that when Rider University has taken over Princeton and Rutgers, and St. Peter's and Fairleigh Dickinson and Trenton State Teachers—a thousand young men and women will have taken their degrees in the study of the early American novel, circa 1950, by diligent study of the novels of John O'Hara, the first novelist lecturer in Rider's history.

They will not have all the answers then, any more than we have many of the answers now. The problems that you face are no easier or more difficult than the problems they will face. By your presence here at Rider you are expressing at least an awareness of a world full of problems, and a willingness to grapple with them. We have that in common—problems. But I have learned, as you will learn, that perfection is not the human condition. Life itself is almost a denial of perfection, even hope is an expression of dissatisfaction; we go on living and hoping, with our life sustained by our hopes, and our hopes directed toward the improvement of the human condition, and the whole thing is the adventure of the pursuit of the unattainable. In New York there used to be a funny little man, who pretty well balanced the good and bad things of the human condition, and every Sunday for a time he would speak to his fellow citizens about the condition of his city, for he was the mayor of the city. He always concluded his broadcasts with a three-word signature that I now repeat: Patience and fortitude.

Speeches

4 ⚼ Writing—What's in It for Me?

While I was trying to put these thoughts down on paper I had a visitor at my apartment. He was a window-cleaner, a Negro window-cleaner, the first one I've ever seen. As a rule in New York the window-cleaners are of Polish extraction. That's one of the small unimportant facts that you pick up as a newspaper reporter that are of very little use to you in later life, unless you happen to be invited to fan the breeze with the members of the Elizabethan Club, and I imagine, or rather I hope, that that honor is bestowed on so few people that facts of that kind may be classified as entirely useless. Anyway, I had a professional visit by a Negro window-cleaner instead of a Pole, and while I don't want to be accused of being a nationalist, or a racist, I think even the anthropology editor of *PM* would admit that there are some differences between the Negro and the Pole. You very seldom get a word out of a Polish window-cleaner beyond a polite Good Morning. I got plenty of words out of this Negro, and some of the words belong in a discussion of my topic, which I may remind you, and at the same time remind myself, is Writing—What's in It for Me? This fat jolly Negro was squeegeeing the window and fascinating my daughter, aged two and a half, when I came home after lunch. *I* said good afternoon, *he* said good afternoon. My daughter said Man Cleaning Window, Hello Man. He said she calls me Man. She oughta be calling me Stupid or Dope. Some people, he went on, they take and leave home ten o'clock in the morning, back home three o'clock

Previously unpublished. John O'Hara spoke to the Elizabethan Club at Yale University in March 1948. His talk is published from the typescript in the Collection of American Literature, The Beinecke Rare Book and Manuscript Library at Yale University. This is the talk referred to on page 32.

55

in the afternoon, sitting around, talking to their little baby, day's work done.

Well, it seemed to give him pleasure, the idea that he was looking at a man who had gone to work at ten in the morning and was back at three in the afternoon. So I let him go on thinking just that. In fact I put on an act for him. I said I'd have been home earlier but my car got stuck in the snow. I have a car, all right, but it's been jacked up since December, and by the way, if there's anybody here this evening who'd like to buy a beautiful, sleek, powerful 1932 Duesenberg, he can see me after the show. I didn't come to New Haven to sell a car, but in just two weeks, two weeks from tomorrow, I'll have more use for dough than I will for a fast car. The car isn't quite fast enough when the e-ternal in-ternal revenue boys start breathing down the back of your neck. I know. But to get back to my window-cleaner friend, as far as he was concerned, the answer to the question, what's in writing for me, would be, the hours are short. The hell you say.

In one form or another, that thought occurs to a lot of people, nonwriting people. How nice, they say, how nice to be your own boss, work when you please, don't have to punch a time clock, knock off whenever you feel like it, and go to Sun Valley, or Hobe Sound, or Placid, or Bermuda, or just sit around "21," getting a load on, having interesting Powers models tickle your feet and so on. I'm afraid that that one illusion is responsible for more brief writing careers than any other single factor. A guy who really has only a talent for whatever they do in Wall Street—admitting for the moment that whatever they do in Wall Street calls for a talent—this guy (and I've known plenty of them) in ideal circumstances is a guy who, if I may repeat myself, *lives* in ideal circumstances. I mean, his family have dough. So along about junior year—sometimes senior year, if he's particularly dull witted—he goes to the old gent, or more usually to Ma, and announces that he'd like to take a whack at writing for two or three years, or whatever the traffic will bear. At the end of two years or three, he says, if I haven't made a successful pitch, I'll give up writing and take a job in the Old Man's Greever Factory making Greevers. Now mind you, I'm not taking a lofty moral attitude about swindling the old man. If the old man is not quite bright, if he hasn't sympathy and perceptiveness enough to know by the time his son reaches, say, twenty, whether the young fellow can or can't write, he ought to be swindled. And my counsel to any undergraduate in this room whose old gent is so lacking in understanding, is take him for as much as you can, as long as you can. At least you'll be keeping the money in the family, temporarily. By the way, I think I ought to mention that this advice comes to you through the courtesy of this speaker, and neither Yale University nor Jergens Lotion assumes any responsibility for the opinions expressed herein.

Of course there's another angle to this swindling deal, and instead of generalizing I'll give you a case in point. I once had a friend, or acquaintance, whose family really were up there in the chips. I don't mean *one* lousy million. I mean Big, Big. If I were to mention his last name I think almost everyone here from the Middle West would recognize it. Certainly everybody from Chicago is familiar with the name. Anyway I was out of a job and another fellow and I went to sponge off our rich friend, who was then a senior at, uh, you know, the college in New Jersey. We spent an agreeable two weeks playing golf and violating the Volstead Act, and what with a little luck at golf and bridge—auction bridge, by the way—I ended up with just about the same ten bucks I had in my kick when I arrived. When I was leaving I thought I ought to show my appreciation to my host, and I wondered what would be the best way to do just that. You can be sure I didn't offer anything in the way of money, and he had a cigarette lighter. He had TEN cigarette lighters. He had *thirty* pairs of shoes. I counted them. I not only wore them, but I *counted* them. So there was one thing I could give him that was unique. *I* could give him *advice.* I'd then been a newspaperman for about five years, and I was hitting the *New Yorker* pretty regularly, so that made me an established writer, or at least *he* thought so, and God knows *I* thought so.

"What are you planning on doing when you get out of college?" I asked him.

"Well," he said, "I think I'd like to write. I think I'd like to write a novel."

"No," I said. "No. Now look here," I said, "I know you've written some nice little things for the Lit, and you're Phi Bete. Like music. Know a lot about it. Good taste and good judgment about painting. Now you've got a chance to be a really important figure in the cultural life of this country." (By the way, this was the spring of 1929.) I said, "All sorts of people are making all sorts of money, and you've got plenty and will have a lot more. Why don't you, instead of futzing around, being a dilettant, maybe writing a half-baked novel or a slim volume of delicate tracery, why don't you have your fun or go to Oxford or both, and then come back and go to work for the old man, but take a position, your rightful position as a businessman and a patron of the arts." At that time there was a lot of bellyaching about our American lack of culture, as usual, and crying the blues because so few men of wealth were doing anything about it.

Well, my rich friend did go to Oxford, stayed there a year, and quit. He remained in Europe, and the next thing I heard about him, he had written a really fine novel. I read it and was full of admiration and envy and at least temporarily a feeling of defeat, or frustration. Rebecca West, for whom I had then and have now a great deal of respect, called my rich friend the most promising young writer since the first book by Scott Fitzgerald, and she wasn't too far wrong.

In all fairness—that is, in all fairness to myself—I admit that my rich friend then discovered Ernest Hemingway, and he wrote a very bad, incredibly bad novel in the manner of Hemingway, and as far as I know he hasn't written another novel since. I haven't seen him since before the war, but I have heard from him through friends. He never went to work for the old man, and never became a patron of the arts. He lives the kind of life that nonwriters think writers live. The house in Bermuda, skiing at the Seigniory, a pied-à-terre in New York. I guess he's an unhappy man, unhappier than most of us. But he wanted to be a writer, and nobody can take that one good book away from him, and maybe one good book is enough. Melville's reputation seems secure.

It's a fact, of course, that you don't have to punch a time clock if you're a free-lance writer, a novelist, or play-wright. But at the risk of being obvious let me say this, the free-lance writer often wishes he did have to punch the clock. In a very serious way, there is a chronometer. It's that calendar, those bills at the beginning of the month. They keep coming. In January I loafed away three weeks in Florida. Even if I could charge off the trip as a legitimate professional expense—and don't think I'm not going to try, because I'll write some stories and make Florida my locale—nevertheless I can't ever get back those three weeks. There's no use kidding myself that I was getting ideas, or getting a much needed rest—although both those items happen to be true. The important thing is that I'm a writer, and I wasn't writing, and when you don't write, the dough doesn't come in. That's why it's tough being your own boss. Nobody can make you write, no-body but you yourself. A sympathetic wife, a nagging wife, an eager bill collector, a tolerant bill collector, a hungry kid—nobody gets those words down but you, and if your heart's not in it, the words are no damn good.

That's about enough on the lure, the attractiveness of the kind of hours writers are supposed to keep. No, one more observation in that connection. There *are* writers, good ones among them, who tell me they get at least a set minimum done every day. Well, I know John Steinbeck pretty well, and I know him to be one of the most serious, painstaking, hard-working craftsmen among the good ones. I also know Ernest Hemingway pretty well, and he works as hard as Steinbeck. They're the best, let's face it. But let's face this, too. When you read a piece about John Steinbeck or Ernest Hemingway, that tells how they start plugging away at eight o'clock in the morning and stay at it till noon or four o'clock, you reach for the salt cellar and sprinkle a few grains on that piece. Steinbeck, the steadier worker of the two, has gone back to work in the last month or two, but if Hemingway is working he's writing with a rifle, the last I heard. When you're writing a novel, or a play, you're a steadier worker than when you're doing short stories or articles, but even a novel that you're all steamed up about doesn't hold you at that desk every single day. The typewriter or the pencil repels you so that you hate the sight of it, and that, my friends, is when you wish you were on somebody's payroll, and not your own boss. What's in it for you? A backache, or a guilty conscience, or both.

As you may have noticed, I've been sneaking up on the part of the answer to my question which has to do with money. To restate the question, What's in It for Me in a pecuniary way?

That's a fair question.

What dough do I get out of it?

Well, I won't go so far as to say that every good writer makes a good living, because there may be good writers that I don't know about, and there may be good writers that I do know about who aren't doing as well as I think they are. But I think it's a safe statement to make that the moment a man writes a good book or a good play he begins to make a decent living from his writing. By a decent living I mean that in a town of four or five thousand he will live on a scale of spending some-somewhat lower than that of the leading doctor and somewhat higher than that of the high school principal. For the moment let's leave Hollywood out of it. A writer whose novel—let's say it's an honest, well-written book, fairly well received—hits 10,000 copies at two dollars and a half a copy, on a 15 percent royalty—that writer will earn $3,750.00. The kind of writer I have in mind should be good for one or two pieces at the *New Yorker*, which would increase his income by a thousand or fifteen hundred dollars, possibly a little more, and certainly more if he should sell more pieces. If this writer is willing *or reluctant but hungry*, he can get more money for stories of the same length at the slicker slicks. An idea for a *New Yorker* story can be tricked up at the end and sold to, for instance, *Collier's* for a dollar a word or better. He might hit *Good Housekeeping* and get two thousand for a short story of 2,000 words. This mythical writer probably has a newspaper or teaching job, and it's a good idea for him to hold on to it until his second and, we hope, better book which, we also devoutly hope, will sell 40 or 50,000. That's a nice living, and our man can go on like that, building up his reputation and therefore his public and his price to magazines for the rest of his good writing days.

He can compromise for eating-money, usually at the expense of his reputation as an artist. The form the com-promise takes is traditionally the writing of hack stuff for the *Saturday Evening Post*, but I'm not sure that that alone ruins a writer. William Faulkner has written a great deal for the *Post*, and Scott Fitzgerald wrote more, and both men bounced back all right. I wish I could do it, but I don't seem to be able to. It's the hardest kind of writing I know of. At least it must be for men like Faulkner and Fitzgerald. Men who write for themselves and one or two other readers. They come to a place in the story where they must make a choice, the choice between saying right out loud, He went to bed with Her. Well, if you're going to sell that story to the *Saturday Evening Post* He *doesn't* go to bed with Her. The story may be illustrated—even in the Post—with pictures of Gwendolyn in the hay, wearing only enough to protect her from the chilly blasts of the postal regulations, and Bertram, the paratrooper that she thought had been killed by the Nazis, Bertram may be seen in the picture, in his pajamas—but if you read the text you will learn that Bertram and Gwendolyn do not get in that bed together, not in the *Saturday Evening Post*. Another favorite—and I've seen this in the *Post*—is a rear view of Gwendolyn stepping into the tub while Bertram may be seen brushing his teeth. But by that time they are good and married, and what Gwendolyn is saying is, "You danced three times with that dreadful Mrs. McCosh at the country club this evening, if I'm not mistaken." You have to read the text to find out what Bertram replied, because with that kind of dialog there isn't room in the caption for his answer. If you are curious to learn what he said, I can tell you this much: he *didn't* say, "And that ain't all I did with Mrs. McCosh," or "Go soak your head." Now you and I, men of the world, know that if Bertram has reached the pajamas stage, and a dish like Gwendolyn is in the hay, Bertram is not going to act like a gentleman and sleep on the living-room couch. Moreover, I have strong doubt that a lady would regard him as a gentleman. Ladies got feelin's, too, you know. We also know that if Gwendolyn, stepping into the tub, picks just that moment to chide Bertram with his attentions to Mrs. McCosh, she *ought* to be told to soak her head, and in real life that's what she *is* told. Well, that's the kind of realism, if Dr. Canby will excuse the expression, that a writer must avoid if he wants to sell stories to the big-paying magazines. It takes skill to avoid it. As far as I'm concerned, it's easier to be honest. But a few writers have that skill, and they employ it with a minimum of compromise.

There are also writers who write nothing but hack stuff, and I have nothing against them. They would be dishonest when they tried to write something else. They simply don't know how to handle realism. They go out for recess and come back with a bloody nose, and it ought to teach them a lesson, not to fool around with those hard-boiled toughies like Hemingway and Steinbeck and—pardon me. But we're not concerned in this paper with the Sax Rohmers, Clarence Budington Kellands, Thomas McMorrows, Faith Baldwins and the other, for want of a better word, commercial hacks. They make their money, and money is what's in it for them.

And as neatly as that I come to the third sub-question and sub-answers. What's in it for me in the way of kudos? Kudos, I don't have to remind you, literally means glory. All right, what's in it for me in the way of glory?

Gentlemen, you've invited the perfect man to answer that question. Me.

I am very much pleased, and honored, to be invited here, to this club, in this university, at this time of my life. I've had many friends in this club, fellows I see in New York, and I suppose if I were to look at the roster from the time the club was founded I would find that I knew a great many more members than I know about. I am not the kind of writer whose manuscripts you'll find back in that rather imposing vault, but just in case you are interested in original O'Hara MSS they're all at Yale, or will be. The MS of my first novel, *Appointment in Samarra*, is temporarily the possession of a lady whose husband is one of Yale's most distinguished alumni, a member of this club, and in her will she has left the MS to the Yale Library. By the way, I use the word manuscript loosely here; literally they are typescripts, as I never write in longhand, but typescript sounds too much like International Business Machines and Thomas J. Watson, so I say manuscript. Anyway, I applaud the action of this club with its classical tastes and traditions, in inviting *living* writers to sound off, and I am happy to be one of those writers who have been so honored.

I am glad to be asked to talk at this club in *this university*. I didn't go to Yale, and neither did my father. He went to Penn in the days when there was a Big Four. As a matter of fact I didn't go to any college, and I guess the only reason I'm sorry I didn't go to college is that I didn't go to Yale. I take a lot of ribbing about that and maybe it *is* a slight case of infantilism, but I can think of worse maladies. I'll tell you a little story about myself. I like to tell the story because by telling it myself I have a theory that I take the curse off it. During the war between the Loyalists and the Franco Fascists, Ernest Hemingway, Vincent Sheean, and James Lardner were on a train bound for Perpignan. Hemingway and Lardner were going to join up with the Loyalists, and Sheean was going to cover the war for a newspaper syndicate. Lardner, you may remember, was killed in that war.

The three of them decided to pool their money and divide it equally, and they did, and they found they had something like two francs left over. They'd all had a few drinks and they got into a serious discussion of what to do with the two francs. Toss it out the window? No, no. Unimaginative. Give it to a porter? No. No good. The porter would think one of the three was a nontipper. Then suddenly—"*I* know what to do with it," said Hemingway. "We'll start a fund to put John O'Hara through Yale."

But I was talking about the kudos in writing, and I described myself as an authority. I am, because I speak from a point of beautiful objectivity. I never have won anything. One year I had a novel that was pretty generally

a critical success and rather agreeably sold enough copies
to enable me to reopen some charge accounts, buy a car,
and generally conduct myself as a thirty-year-old bachelor
ought to conduct himself. Somewhere between disgraceful and discreet. The following spring I made furtive inquiries about the date of the announcement of the Pulitzer
Prize. I knew it was always on a Monday, but I wanted to
make sure of the exact date, because I planned to be out of
town that day. Why? Modesty. I had been led to believe—not only by myself—that my novel stood a pretty
good chance of winning the Pulitzer Prize. But I could
have saved myself the trouble. When the announcements
came, the novel prize was given to a book about an old
lady who chewed tobacco and said God damn. I had some
people that said God damn in my novel, but nobody that
chewed tobacco, not even a man that chewed tobacco, so
naturally I wasn't eligible that year. The next year I did
have a novella in which there were some people who
chewed tobacco, but they were coal miners, not old
ladies, and anyway a novella is a special short form, and
the people who give prizes for novels—let this be a lesson
to you—want something substantial. After that Mondays
in May were just like other Mondays to me.

I also used to think I wrote a pretty good country short
story, and one year I had eleven stories in the commended
or honorable mention list, I forget what he called it, in the
late E. J. O'Brien's annual book. It seemed to me that I was
a breeze to win the O. Henry Prize, which is a rather
attractive one thousand bucks. But as long as I've been
writing short stories—twenty years—I've never won so
much as an ashtray, and I'm a heavy smoker.

What about the theatre? There's the Pulitzer Prize, the
Critics Circle Prize, the Donaldson award, which is something given by *Billboard* magazine, and several other
prizes. I had written a musical comedy which, with some
not too startling exceptions, enjoyed an excellent press,

and also ran a year. Well, this time I had a middle-aged woman who said God damn, but I couldn't see her chewing tobacco. I was tempted to have her smoke cigars, because that would have been in character, but I remember that years ago I had seen Helen Westley in a play in which she smoked cigars, and that was all I could remember of the play, and I wanted my show to be remembered for something else. So I tossed away my chances of the Pulitzer Prize. But even the Critics Circle gave me only two votes: one by my best friend, and the other by a man I don't know at all, but he was shortly afterward fired from his paper.

I've even aspired to a movie Oscar. I wrote a picture for Jean Gabin, which wasn't too bad even after the members of the Twentieth Century-Fox Elizabethan Club got through with it, and it was mentioned as one of the Ten Best of the Year by the eminent scholar, Yale man, and, I must add, drinking companion, Howard Barnes. But no Oscar.

And there you have it. No prizes. Nevertheless I am writing a novel, nevertheless I go on writing short stories, nevertheless I have finished the first draft of a play. I am doing these things because they're my job, my work, at which I earn my living. And best of all, I am doing what I like to do. On the way up on the train I was reading in Mr. *Luce's* magazine—great fellow, Yale tycoon, fired me in 1929—I was reading about an organization that tells whether you are fit for an executive job by, among other things, having you study pictures, particularly one picture of a gymnast who was either climbing or descending a rope. It was up to you to decide which the gymnast was doing, going up, or coming down, and if you answered correctly, you are an executive type. . . . I took the test fairly, no peeking, and gentlemen, I have an announcement to make: I am not an executive type! I said the fellow was coming down, the organization says he was climbing up.

Now I could give that organization a hell of an argument about that picture, but perhaps the very fact that I would be disposed to argue would indicate that I am not the executive type. The executive type, according to my experience of them, and it's been plenty, the executive type is a whip-cracking son of a gun when it comes to giving orders, but he must also be proficient in the repeated vertical gesture of the skull, and familiar with the words si, oui, ja, da, and by-all-means-chief. I am not the executive type.

I also came across another gem, this time in the *Saturday Evening Post*. I quote: "An FBI agent addressing a group of fingerprint men remarked that anyone who wanted to paint a picture, compose a song or write a story had no business in law-enforcement work."

So there go two lines of endeavor out the window: I can't be an executive, and there is no place for me in law-enforcement work. Thank the good Lord!

But the funny thing is, the FBI is right, and so are the executive-screeners, or whatever they are. If you find yourself being a writer, a creative writer of course, going your own way, you are the reverse of the FBI man, who on the obverse is committed to the enforcing of rules that he did not write and may not even thoroughly understand. And before you reach for the telephone let me remind you that Stalin's recent blast against Prokofief and Katchatourian isn't anything new; the Russian intellectuals have been on the way out for years. They have served their purpose. In this country I don't think the intellectuals have ever been *in*, but now they're out all over. You may, as an intellectual, dream up a new system, or modifications in the existing system, but you do that yourself, and when it comes time to enforce the changes you have to call in the FBI type. And by the FBI type I have time to explain only that I mean, NOT anyone who wants to paint a picture, compose a song, or write a story. And NOT the executive type. It might be interesting to give an FBI agent the executive-type test; my guess is that he'd pass *cum laude*. And anyone in this room who is, as they say, thinking of becoming a writer might take an FBI or executive test, and if *he* passes he'd better start taking a lot more math, and Econ courses. Of course you can take some of those tests with your left hand, so to speak: you put down the answers that are the opposite of what you feel, just for the fun of beating the test. If that's your idea of fun.

Now I haven't really been straying away from the subject of the rewards of writing, particularly kudos. A writer—and I think I include all the other artists except actors, who can be artists—the writer's rewards are different in *kind* from the rewards that a nonartist appreciates. All these remarks may be obvious enough, but the obvious isn't going to do you any good if it hasn't been stated, by you or someone else, and the obvious isn't going to do you any harm unless it's stated too often by someone else or, if you're a writer, by you. The most truly satisfactory reward a writer ever gets is the moment he holds that book in his hand and says, This is my baby. You can have that in degrees (and I don't mean honorary degrees). Your first words in type, then your first by-line, provided the copy desk hasn't made you ashamed of what follows under the by-line. And then after your first, or maybe your tenth or fifteenth book is published, to get a really ecstatic review. But take it from one who has wept tears of joy over an understanding, sympathetic, favorable review—the joy is ephemeral. You can always go back, reread that wonderful review, and while you may find some felicitous phrase that you'd forgotten, you'll also find that that friendly, understanding, sympathetic reviewer left something out. He may have compared you with Hemingway or Walter Pater, and that's not bad, and he may have said you were better than Hemingway or Walter Pater, which isn't bad and isn't likely, but then why didn't he also say you were better than Ring Lardner and Trollope, and was he woolgathering when he read the passage about Dwight and Ermintrude on the Empire State Building? Why didn't he say something about that? Tristan and Isolde, indeed. In other words, the critic can't win. Nobody ever can tell you how good that book was if you know it was good yourself, and you have your reward when you hold the book in your hand. It is an accomplished fact and it is yours. The Pulitzer Prize people, the Book-of-the-Month people, and the critic for the Macon, Georgia, *Tribune*, may bestow their various kisses on it, but in your heart you will be saying, "And why not?" And you yourself? Harvard may give you an honorary degree, and the Wesleyan chapter of Phi Beta Kappa may provide you with something for your watch chain that your alma mater neglected to provide, and you may find yourself bewildered in the Academy of Arts and Letters—mind you, I'm speaking only from vicarious experience—but upon receiving any or all of these honors I imagine your secret, ungracious response will be "I'm only the same guy I was before I wrote the book," although of course you're not the same guy, and never will be again. For better or for worse, most likely for better, you are a writer.

First book or tenth book, regardless of when the kudos come to you, or even if they don't come to you, you're a writer, and you're stuck with it. That goes for the rich young man I spoke of earlier. I'm sure he still regards himself as a writer, even though he may have retired to a fashionable club, or has become an Egyptologist, a radio announcer, a book critic, a member of the state legislature, or piano player in a house of ill repute. I know, and more importantly, he knows that the high point of his life was when he hefted that first novel and whatever its weight, appraised it as invaluable. What may have driven him out of the practice of writing is the loneliness of it. I suppose that's why so many of us work at night, when a man can be ideally alone. Novels have been written in the city room of a newspaper, with forty typewriters banging away, the press association printers thumping away, reporters shouting "Boy! Copy!" and the presses singing. Under those conditions the writer is alone too; he just isn't ideally alone. Ideally alone I suppose is any place of quiet without disturbance, and the closest approximation to that in the city is at three or four in the morning, provided the baby isn't getting any new teeth and the sixteen-year-old girl upstairs isn't employing that shining hour to smooth over the rough spots in her rendition of Ravel's *Bolero*. You have to do your work alone, literally, and consequently it is right and proper that the true rewards, the most satisfactory ones, should be the approval that no one else can give you. Your artistic conscience will withhold the kudos sometimes after Harvard has said Well Done.

You know this very club was started with some of the spirit of loneliness and, of course, accompanying nonconformist attitude that I've been talking about. One of the founders of the Elizabethan Club has told me that he honestly thinks he was asked to join because he was the only man in Yale University who had a piano in his room. Incidentally, as an outsider and a guest I hope I am permitted to remark that he was the only man ever to display another special kind of independence: he resigned from Skull and Bones. So you gentlemen here tonight owe something to the independence of lonely spirit that caused a man to keep a piano in his room and ride horseback in a day when football was king, and I think I ought to add that "Bulldog," or maybe it was "Bingo," was created on that same piano. In other words, the thing that makes a man want to paint a picture, compose a song, or write a story is responsible for the founding and continued existence of the Elizabethan Club.

And I think we've done very well.

Thank you.

5 ◢ What Makes a Writer?

A couple of weeks ago, when I told a friend of mine that I was going to speak at Rutgers, he looked at me with some alarm and said: "You better look out. You may be starting a new career." He was referring to the fact, which he is aware of, that since last September I have read papers at Princeton and Lawrenceville, and that I also have agreed to read a paper at the University of Illinois in June. To put it another way, in this one year I will have given more talks than in the forty-five previous years of my life, and, as I say, he viewed me with alarm. Old authors never die, they only talk for pay.

Well, my friend, who by the way is a drama critic, which disproves the widely held theory that drama critics have no friends—this man kidded me about my new career, but after a little while he made a profound statement. He said: "As a matter of fact, if there must be speeches, I'd rather make them than listen to them."

Fine words from a drama critic. Rather revealing. They may help to prove another widely held theory, namely, that drama critics are either frustrated playwrights or rebuffed actors.

Now I have given some thought to my friend's remark,

Previously unpublished. John O'Hara spoke to the English Club at Rutgers University on 2 May 1953. His talk is published from the typescript at the Rutgers University Library. The title has been supplied by the editor.

and at this point I can only say that at *this very minute* I'd rather be *listening* to a speech than giving *this* one. If an author turned speechmaker is at all conscientious—and I'm nothing if not conscientious—he should be informative, instructive, or, if possible, both. But how to be informative or instructive?

I am the greatest, and sometimes I think the *only* authority on this particular author. I could go on for hours about myself and my work. Indeed, I could go on for hours about myself without ever touching upon my work. But such an autobiographical orgy, just like any other kind of orgy, requires at least one other participant, and after a few hundred words I'm afraid I would find myself talking to empty chairs.

As I wrote these words I found myself talking to empty chairs, and it is not my idea of fun.

So then, if I am going to be informative perhaps I had better be informative on another subject. Well, I tossed and turned and I decided not to talk to you about the quantum theory, or beekeeping, or the sport of curling, or the state of Texas. I have my own quantum theory, taken from the Latin. Stated in two words it is "How much?" On beekeeping I am not an authority. In fact for about fifteen years I have been having an occasional drink with a very dapper fellow whom I would run into at the bar of "21." ("21," by the way, is my chief connection with Rutgers.) He and I would chat about the trivial things you talk about with a casual bar acquaintance, and I never knew what the fellow did for a living. In fact, I didn't think he did *any*thing. He dressed like a man that didn't do anything. But one day a couple of years ago I ran into him and he said: "I was hoping I'd find you. I've brought you a copy of my new book." Holy hell, I thought the guy's another author. Well, he *was*, all right, but *what* he was was author of a standard work on—you guessed it—beekeeping.

My information on the sport of curling is fairly limited.

It is played on a bonspiel, by men who wear tam-o'-shanters and carry brooms and highballs. Next winter I may have more to say on the sport of curling, and I will be glad to come to New Brunswick. Unless, of course, Scotty Cameron has already stolen my thunder. Curling is very popular where he comes from.

On the other hand, I have a vast fund of information on the state of Texas and Texans, but in mixed company I would have to be less explicit than an adequate treatment of the subject demands, so Texas is out.

Texas is out. Beekeeping is out, curling belongs in another season of the year, and while I may sneak in a few autobiographical details, I have rejected myself as the principal topic for the evening. What else am I left with? I know a thing or two about music, especially American jazz music. I know a thing or two about sports and sports personalities, and about horsemanship and horses. As a matter of fact I am leaving tomorrow for the Kentucky Derby, and I confidently expect to make my expenses through my knowledge of horses. I also find that I know a thing or two about railroading, and about the motion picture business and show business and the newspaper business. But I concede that there are other men who know more about all of these activities, except possibly the newspaper business and the men and women in it.

Still, I don't think I was invited here to talk about the newspaper business. I was given carte blanche, and Mr. Hamilton made it very easy for me, or tried to make it very easy for me, by suggesting that I could even read selected passages from my own prose. Now that tempted me, because last summer I started to reread a passage of my own prose, and before I went to bed I had reread the whole book. For the first time in seventeen years, by the way.

But at least Mr. Hamilton gave me a lead. I began to think of writing, and from there I went on to thinking of writers, and in a kind of impersonal, contemplative way, I began to think of what makes a writer.

That's really what I want to talk about, and around, this evening.

What makes a writer? How, in the slang of the 1920s, does he get that way?

Now let me say at this point that I don't think I'm going to arrive at anything much, but I hope it will be interesting to you and to me to have a look at some writers and wonder how they got that way.

They tell a story—and they, whoever they are, tell it much better than I do—about Bertrand Russell and John Strachey.

Strachey, of course, was one of the big-domed intellectuals before he became more active in English politics, and before that he was a gentleman. I mean, simply, the English gentleman, the public school boy and Oxford-or-Cambridge, I forget which, man. In the ordinary course of events he might have been expected to join a couple of good London clubs, participate in the London night life, the weekends in the country, and possibly even stand for Parliament when he had sown an oat or two. But he didn't happen to be that kind of person. He was serious-minded from the start, and one thing he was terribly serious-minded about was his admiration for Bertrand Russell, who, of course, is a belted earl, and if anything more highly situated in the social scale than Strachey.

The day came when Strachey was able to wangle his first meeting with Russell, and—so the story goes—Strachey went to Russell's country place for the meeting, full of awe and trepidation, and wondering what to say to the old man.

He needn't have worried.

He was ushered into Bertrand Russell's study, and the

old boy, knowing all about Strachey's background, and, possibly, everything else, said to Strachey, without rising: "I didn't like my father. What was your trouble?"

Now I'm not going to attempt to go very deeply into the Freudian depths of six or seven authors that I have in mind, but as much for my own information as yours I am going to take six or seven authors, all of whom I know pretty well, and perhaps by stating a few facts or semifacts about them all, we might discover something or things common to all or most of them.

I will take, for my purpose, Ernest Hemingway, John Steinbeck, F. Scott Fitzgerald (by the way, there are a lot of people calling him Scott Fitzgerald today that never, in my estimation, should have come close enough to call him *Mister* Fitzgerald), and William Faulkner. Four novelists. And three playwrights. Philip Barry, Thornton Wilder, and Clifford Odets.

I have looked at that list a dozen times, quickly and slowly, to see if I couldn't discover an obvious common characteristic. And to tell you the truth, there isn't one. These seven happen to be, most likely, the seven I admire most—although I might make a somewhat different list next week.

What common background did they have? Well, none. Hemingway's father was a physician, but the only one of the seven. Steinbeck and Wilder were the sons of schoolteachers, and in Wilder's case, a teaching missionary. Fitzgerald's father was in trade and so was Odets'. Faulkner's father was a farmer, and Barry's father died when Barry was an infant, and Barry was raised by an older brother.

Five of these men went to college. I don't mean they all got degrees, but from Steinbeck, who went to California or Stanford very briefly, we proceed to Fitzgerald, who did a fair stretch at Princeton, to Faulkner, who went to the University of Mississippi and, I seem to recall, to Oxford in England,[1] not Mississippi, for a short while; then we move on to Barry, who did get a degree at Yale and went to Harvard for the English 47 Workshop, and finally to Wilder, who started at Oberlin, got a degree at Yale, and since then had studied at the Sorbonne and Harvard and every place else, and is, in fact, enjoying professorial status at Harvard right now. Hemingway and Odets never got to college at all. So, between Steinbeck, who went to Stanford for part of freshman year, we get all the changes right through to Thornton Wilder, who really is never very far from the odor of academic sanctity.

We therefore prove nothing about college. Wilder, with all the caps and gowns a man will ever need, can't do things that Odets can do, and Odets, out of Morris High School, hasn't the ready erudition that Wilder has, and that's only the negative way of putting it. You can put it positively if you prefer.

Let's try another customarily important influence. Religion. There we have less in common than on the collegiate evaluation. Barry and Fitzgerald were born Roman Catholics, and Hemingway was a convert to the Catholic Church, but Odets was born a Jew, and Wilder, Steinbeck, and Faulkner were brought up as Protestants of various denominations. Counting Hemingway as a Catholic, which I should think might be stretching a point, the score on religion is three, three, and one, and there again we prove nothing.

Very well. Let's try a very obvious thing: physical structure. Well, Fitzgerald, Faulkner, Barry, and Wilder are all in the definitely short or medium-sized classification. Hemingway and Steinbeck are big men, and Odets is somewhere between Steinbeck and Wilder.

I discover that we can come a little closer to a common

---

1. Faulkner did not attend Oxford.

characteristic if we examine the temperament of these men. I have taken as a standard the characteristic that we commonly call quick-tempered. Without much hesitancy I conclude that the only one of the seven who is not quick-tempered is Faulkner. Now of course I'm not saying that his not being quick-tempered made him a writer, any more than I am saying that the other six are writers because they are quick-tempered, and I also must tell you that quick-tempered does not necessarily mean that Thornton Wilder would punch you in the nose as quickly as one of the others might. But that's only a matter of degree of action, not of spontaneity. And so I offer this statistic for what you want to make of it in your past and future comparative studies of these artists.

There is only one thing that I think they all have in common, and yet I hesitate to designate it as more than a superficially observed phenomenon, because I have to make an exception. First, I will put it this way: not one of these men was the son of wealth. I will go further and say that not one was the son of small-town wealth. In other words, if you were to go by New York, Boston, and Philadelphia standards, the word wealth would not enter into it at all. The kind of people who owned yachts in the boyhood and young manhood of the seven authors we are dealing with. Fitzgerald, of course, observed wealth closely all his life, and so did Hemingway most of his life. As a matter of strong probability, Hemingway has known more *richer* people than Fitzgerald did, and Barry knew more of them than Hemingway *and* Fitzgerald, and really knew them better, because his life was almost entirely with the rich. He *lived* with the rich, which is something different from playing with the rich when the rich felt like playing, which was the case with Fitzgerald and Hemingway. But all this is secondary influence.

What I started out to say was that these seven authors were not in the beginning members of the rich, but what I want to add very emphatically is that neither were they members of the poor. They all went to high school—not one of them went to preparatory boarding school, *any* preparatory boarding school,[2] let alone Groton or St. Marks. But they all did go to high school, and at the time they were all growing up, really poor boys didn't go to high school. Fitzgerald was brought up among luxuries, and I know that Barry lived in what was known as a nice part of Rochester, New York, and he went to dancing school with the rich. Hemingway's family had enough money to have a distant place to go to in the summer, and I can personally testify that a small-town physician's family usually live very well, so long as the old gent is alive and able to practice. Odets is deliberately mysterious about his financial background, or used to be when I knew him well, but once in a while he would drop a remark that inadvertently revealed that as a growing boy he was not from hunger. And as to the teachers' sons, you all know, or should know, that teachers QUOTE manage somehow UNQUOTE. They shouldn't have to, but they do.

Now just as everything gets kind of cozy, and I am prepared to group all these authors under the classification of good old middle class, along comes this fellow Faulkner again, and easy-going Bill, with his slow temper, makes me want to lose mine. For, the fact of the matter is, William Faulkner, although certainly not the son of wealth, was nevertheless one of the landed gentry, and I am far from sure that I can place him among the great middle class. He didn't have money, but he wasn't poor. You might say it's a question of attitude, attitude that you strike so early in life that money has practically nothing to do with it. It isn't even solely and peculiarly Southern. It may be more pronounced in the Southern[er], because in

2. Fitzgerald went to the Newman School for two years.

the South that Faulkner grew up in, everyone, white or
Negro, knew who the landed gentry were, in spite of the
disconcerting fact that the landed gentry often didn't have
any land. I'm afraid that I cannot say with firm conviction
that brought up as he was, Faulkner belonged to the
middle class socially, no matter what the family rating
might have been financially. I suppose I'll have to leave it
with my earlier remark that none of these men, Faulkner
included, belonged to families that had ocean-going
yachts.

So let's try something else. Ah, yes. All good American
stock. All native-born Americans. But then Wilder comes
in to louse that up. Wilder was born in China.

It may just be, ladies and gentlemen, that there is no
answer to that question of mine, what makes a writer. At
least no answer that we can get at in a once-over-lightly
like this. I think we are on fairly safe ground when we
assert that the very rich don't breed writers. We are on
fairly safe ground if we don't venture beyond that limited
statement. But—and this is kind of a parenthetical remark, don't think they don't breed would-be writers. I
don't want to attempt to give the impression that I live
with the rich, but I'd be just as big a phony if I were to
pretend I don't know a lot of rich people, and believe me,
one of the saddest discoveries you will make in the homes
of great wealth is the privately printed family history, or
privately printed book of poems, or privately printed
book of exploration. No matter when they actually *were*
written, they all read as though they had been written at
least a century ago. Written by cultured people, of sound
eighteenth-century education, and written for cultured
people, of sound eighteenth-century education, and pref-
erably related within the third degree of kindred. There
are plenty of them who want to write, and there is an
occasional one who can write with some grace, but they
do not grow up with any compulsion to write and there-

fore they haven't the *time* to write because they are not forced to *find* the time, say after doing a trick on rewrite or the copy desk, or in an advertising agency, or a four-hour watch on the bridge of a tramp steamer, or wherever it is real writers flee from in order to get to their real work. Even Henry James and Edith Wharton fled from home in order to get to their real work.

I am reluctant to bring out that old square peg, or misfit theory, but I honestly don't see how it can be avoided. It's what I believe. We all get a little tired of reading about authors on the jackets of their books: after finishing three years of high school, he was deckhand on a Great Lakes oreboat and from there made his way to Cape Town, South Africa, and following a short spell as gunrunner he returned to the United States and spent four years as a reporter on various newspapers, etc. I have known many men with careers that read like that, who can't write their way out of a high school composition, but on the other hand, I am usually pessimistic when I read on the jacket of a book that the author went to Hotchkiss and Yale and spent a year at Oxford before settling down to write this, his first novel. And after ten pages of the gentleman's book my pessimism is all too well justified.

I am not urging you who want to write to scamper out of this room and hop the next rattler or have an illegitimate child. But I do say—well, *what* do I say?

I say write it, good luck, and good night.

6 ⚑ The Prize Is a Good One

This is the first time that a book of mine has won a prize, so I cannot say now that I have been caught unprepared: after all, I've been waiting almost twenty-two years.

The prize is a good one. In my case any prize is a good one, but this one is particularly good because it represents the judgment of people who make books, as distinguished from those who can, and sometimes do, break them. As an author I am in some ways closer to the publishers and manufacturers and sellers of books than I am to the people who pass literary judgment. The publishers, the manufacturers, the sellers of books, and the authors have, together, more at stake than the men and women who review books. But I'm afraid that what it finally comes down to is that the author is really on his own, since the publishers, the manufacturers, and the sellers of books are not limited to one chance a season. The author is so limited to one chance and indeed, he is lucky, and industrious, if he has one chance every three seasons.

I am taking the liberty of accepting the National Book Award not only for my current novel, *Ten North Frederick*, published by Random House, price three-ninety-five, but at least to some extent a recognition of the fact, and I immodestly call it a fact, that since 1934 I have been publishing novels and books of short stories in which I told as honestly as I could what I have seen, heard, thought, and felt about a great many of the men and women who populate this country. At the time of writing I first have to satisfy myself that I am telling the truth, then that I am telling it in the most readable, by my standards, fashion I know. I am immodest enough to believe that the opinion of posterity is the least of my worries, and should be the least for anyone who writes about contemporary life. I say that because I have written so accurately and so honestly that my overall contribution will have to be

Previously unpublished. John O'Hara received the National Book Award for *Ten North Frederick* on 7 February 1956. His acceptance speech is published from the typescript through the courtesy of the Pennsylvania State University Libraries. The title has been supplied by the editor.

considered by future students of my time. My lack of humility on this point is due not to arrogance but to conviction, since already in my lifetime two of my earlier novels have become works of reference, which happen to be catalogued under Fiction instead of under History. But I hope you will pardon my irreverence when I remind you that if they took the fiction out of history, history would be in a hell of a way. Almost as badly off as if they took the history out of fiction.

My friend Richardson Dilworth, an experienced campaigner, recently was elected mayor of Philadelphia, and I went to the inauguration ceremony. When it came time for him to make his speech, he choked up and for a minute could not proceed. Finally he was able to say: "As my opponent said, I am an emotional man." I am an emotional man too, more pleased than I dare tell you with this award from the members of my own trade, what might easily be called the National Book Reward. I am pleased, too, because it pleases my family and my friends, including some friends I never have met. At this time I would like to make one request, which I shall put in the form of an expressed hope: I hope you will ask me again.

I thank you.

7 ✒ Remarks on the Novel

In view of the fact that there has been no announcement of the subject of my discourse this evening, you will forgive me if I am immodest enough to suspect that you

John O'Hara delivered the Gertrude Clarke Whittal lecture at the Library of Congress on 14 January 1957, at the time when an attempt was being made to suppress *Ten North Frederick* in Detroit. His lecture was first published in *Three Views of the Novel* (Washington, D.C.: The Library of Congress, 1957) under the auspices of the Gertrude Clarke Whittal Poetry and Literature Fund.

came here out of curiosity, curiosity about me, and about what shocking, or provocative, or entertaining, or stimulating, or instructive things I might have to say. To some extent that curiosity has already been satisfied, in a matter of seconds. You see before you an American author, six feet tall, 195 pounds, grey at the temples, two weeks short of fifty-two years of age, obviously unaccustomed to public speaking, afflicted with an Eastern Pennsylvania twang, writer of several best-sellers, writer also of an equal number of non-sellers, occasionally banned in Detroit, Michigan, Akron, Ohio, and East Germany; and almost completely ill at ease on the platform.

For those whose curiosity can be so easily satisfied I now suggest a quick and quiet departure, and I make that suggestion with no bitterness, without prejudice—and indeed, with some envy. After all, this is "I Love Lucy" night, and I am also under the impression that it is the night when the quiz program called "21" appears at a new time and on a different network. I make mention of the latter because it will give those who leave us the opportunity to see Carl Van Doren's nephew being just as nervous as I am—at, I may say, considerably greater profit. I wonder if those of you who have watched that program have given any thought to the comments Benjamin Franklin is making to Uncle Van Doren. Carl Van Doren has been in heaven long enough to have made the acquaintance of Mr. Franklin and to have straightened out the differences that inevitably would come up when biographer finally meets biographee; and if heaven is everything they say it is, they must be enjoying unlimited television, and I would give a lot to hear Franklin's remarks on thrift when the younger and live Van Doren is torturing himself with his decisions as to whether or not to go on. But notwithstanding the enlightenment I offer this evening, I am obviously unable to reproduce for you the Franklin epigrams, so I shall ask those of you who are remaining to put aside the scene I have created and return with me to Washington, D.C., and these hallowed precincts.

For I have just as much curiosity about you as you have about me. I am most certainly not going to ask you to turn to your neighbor on your right and introduce yourself. This is an informal talk, but let's not get carried away with the spirit of informality. Let's keep the informality to this side of the lectern. I would not think of asking you to join me in "Old McDonald Had a Farm," or "Down By the Old Mill Stream," and I think we'll all be happier in the long run if we limit ourselves to an occasional chuckle or a burst of applause when I have sent home a point. If we get through the evening *without* the occasional chuckle, and *without* the burst of applause, *I* can always blame it on the acoustics—and *you* can blame it on the people at the Library, who didn't have sense enough to hold Irving Stone over for a second week. Parenthetically, I have been a little troubled by Mr. Stone's appearance here. I like Irving. I have been to his house and he has been to mine when we both lived in California. But what do you suppose was in the minds of the committee when they scheduled the author of *Lust for Life* to precede the author of *A Rage to Live?* Coincidence? Well, maybe. And close parentheses. I was saying that I have as much curosity about you as you have about me.

You have no idea how strongly tempted I am to ask that lady, that gentleman, that lady, that gentleman, what their names are, what they do for a living, where you live, what you did this afternoon, what you're going to do tomorrow, and so on. There is hardly anyone I know in this room this evening. And yet for all I know, there are two people in this room now, who don't know each other, who will leave here without meeting each other, but if *I* were to meet them separately, it could easily come to pass that I would put them together in a novel or a play. It could come to pass, although not so easily, that in among you tonight there are a man and a woman whom I could put together much more permanently than a man and a woman are joined together in actual life. By which, of course, I mean no more and no less than that I might create two characters who would outlive us all. And the ultimate, of course, would be if I got really good and put together a man and a woman who would go down in literary history with Tristan and Isolde, or Romeo and Juliet—or Frankie and Johnny.

Then, too, there are quite possibly two people in this room who, I hope, will not meet, whom a competent novelist could put together to create a classic murder story. I am not opposed to classic murder stories, but sometimes life does mirror Art, and I don't want to leave here with blood on my hands.

I now have given you a glimpse of the novelist at work, and, rather sneakily, I have eased myself into my topic for the evening, which, somewhat to the surprise of no one, is: The Novel.

At the beginning I should admit, or confess, or simply state that there is probably no one in this room who is more than thirty years old, who has not read more novels than I have. Among my friends, among the people I see the most, there is a constantly surprising number—surprising *by* their number—of men who earn their living in Wall Street, or Broad Street, or Devonshire Street, who are therefore businessmen, and glad of it, who are at the same time so much more cultured than I that it is I who am more likely to be on the defensive in cultural matters than they. Now here let me quickly say that, in spite of Sinclair Lewis and my good friend the late Philip Barry, I do not believe that there is a very large number of frustrated authors and artists among our commercial men. When a foremost intellect like Thornton Wilder comes to my house I am honored and delighted to be in his company, but when inevitably he speaks the name of Sören Aabye Kierkegaard or the somewhat easier to pronounce name of Franz Kafka, I want to send out a hurry call for any of a half-dozen guys who never have written so much as a bad parody for the *Bawl Street Journal*. The incidence of cultural interest among businessmen has not yet reached proportions that should alarm any of us, but my mention of those who do read, and read a lot, and read what are acceptably called the best things, serves the double purpose of publicly refuting the intellectual snobbishness about the whole race of businessmen—and of publicly stating that if I am to be judged by my reading, I cannot be called an intellectual.

That is not to say that I don't read. I have passed a great deal of time in poolrooms and saloons, it is true, but not lately. And all my life I have managed to pay a great deal of attention to the printed word. But my reading habits are such that I am surprised that I have been able to read as many books as I have, considering the amount of reading I do and have done in the newspapers and magazines. By the look of things the newspapers and magazines are fast relinquishing their hold on me, what with the total disappearances and mergers that continue to occur. But while there are magazines and newspapers, they will have first claim on my reading interest.

Now when I make that admission, which, by the way I don't always make so freely, since I have found it not at all difficult to fake culture at a dinner party—indeed, it can be fun to see how well you can fake knowledge of a book, a play, a painting, or a symphony without getting yourself into trouble—when I make that admission, forthrightly as I am doing now, the layman, that is to say, the nonwriter, is usually astounded. "You mean to say you haven't read *The Nun's Story* or *Bridey Murphy*, or whatever is under discussion? I should think you'd have to read everything." Well, one of the most obvious answers to that is that if I read half of everything, or an even smaller fraction, my own contribution to American letters would be considerably curtailed—a notion, by the way, that has occurred to more than one critic, not excluding some in this very town. My real excuse though, and no matter how lame it sounds, is that I haven't got the time. I read the newspapers and fact-pieces in the magazines very quickly. My experience on newspapers and magazines is vast. I've never been a copyboy, and I've never been a publisher, but I have done everything else on the editorial side, from covering girls' field hockey to a Congressional investigation, and I'm afraid that neither our girls nor our Congressmen are at their best in those circumstances. If you have done as much writing in journalism as I have done, you can run through, without skipping, a long piece because in many instances it is almost as though you had done it yourself. A straight, really compact, news story—let's say a disaster of some kind—does not and should not allow for elegant literary exercises. The restrictions on magazine articles are looser and fewer, but even in them I read at a pretty rapid pace, because regardless of the style that the by-line encourages, I am not reading for aesthetic reasons. I am reading for information first, and style—oh, how many Rebecca Wests are there?

But when I read a novel I read it almost as though I were looking at it through a jeweler's loupe. I hope I don't move my lips when I am reading a novel, but anyone who stood behind me and watched how slowly I turn the pages would expect to see my jaw going up and down as I carefully pushed my gnarled finger from one word to the next. One time in the country I watched a fellow, who was not a great reader, try to entertain himself with a best seller while the rain was keeping him off the golf course. Someone—I'm afraid the someone was me—said: "Look at Jack fighting a book." It was hell for the poor guy. He would look down at it as if he were in a geology class and had been given a hunk of rock to study. Then he would remember that it was a book and his eyes would focus on the print. The eyes and the head would go back and forth as though he were a spectator at a very *tiny* tennis match. Then he would sigh, look out to see what the damned rain was doing, and finally lay the book on his knee and yield to the sandman. It was a northeaster, three days, and poor miserable Jack had done just two pages—I counted—by the time the sun came out.

I am a little faster than that, but not much. I distrust all similes and metaphors, but when I read a novel by the *good* men I am at work. Mind you, I get pleasure out of work. I work hard and constantly, but whatever pleasure I get out of it, it is serious, serious work. My hard-playing, ten-goal days are over, and I'm not a bit sorry. In this respect, if in very few others, I am like my father. My father was a surgeon in a small town in Pennsylvania. He didn't drink, he didn't even smoke. But every week, every Wednesday, he took the train to Philadelphia, a hundred miles away, and spent the hours from eleven A. M. to four P. M. watching John B. Deaver perform surgical operations. I don't know enough about surgery to be able to tell the difference between brilliance and clumsiness, but I never have any trouble recognizing the skill of a Hemingway or a Steinbeck or a Faulkner. I am not like you who don't write, or most of you who write literary criticism. You can be satisfied with the emotional experience and the intellectual stimulation, and that is quite enough if you are not a critic. If you have bought or been given a novel by Ernest Hemingway you are going to read it for pleasure, and when you have finished reading it, you have had that pleasure, regardless of how much you did or did not like the book. But when *I* read a novel by Ernest Hemingway, I have had that pleasure and something more. I know, because I am a man, that I have had a pleasurable experience; I know, because I am an author, what Hemingway did and did not do that caused me to have that experience. I can see where an extra speech would have loused up a scene told in dialog, and where one extra noun of description would have been one noun too much. Sure, that extra speech and that extra noun do get in sometimes, and I want to say, "Now, Ernest, you shouldn't have." Or, "I wish you had put *that* in," when I have found something lacking. But when I critize one of the good ones unfavorably I try not to criticize him on a basis of what *I* would do but of what *he* should have done or not done. I am not Ernest Hemingway, a vital statistic for which we both thank God. I am not Steinbeck or Faulkner. I am me, content to be me. As the Frenchmen say in a quite different context, "Vive la différence!" But I want and expect them to be at their best always, and I am heartily pleased when they are successful because I am on their side, because they care about words. And words are like all the other things that are available to you, that can help you or hurt you. When the good men are successful I am encouraged too.

A moment ago you heard me say, "regardless of how much you did or did not like the book." I would like to use that as a sort of text, but first I also would like to say that at this stage of my remarks I am using Hemingway only because he is the obvious symbol for author, as a few years ago I might have used Joe Di Maggio as a symbol for baseball player, even in this highly partisan American League town. In the past in interviews I have said, and not been misquoted, that a man or a woman who buys one of my books has a perfect right to put the knock on it, just as a man who had bought a Pierce-Arrow was fully entitled to say he bought a lemon. He even had the right to say he preferred the Peerless or the Marmon or the Winton. (I hope you notice how carefully I am placing this analogy in the remote past.) I still say he has that right. If he has bought my book, he has done business with me and he becomes either a satisfied or a dissatisfied customer. I am less tolerant of the people who deal with lending libraries: they pay a few pennies, of which I get nothing, and knock the book; or they like the book but won't buy it. There is now just about nobody who can't afford to buy a book he likes. Be that as it may, while I uphold the buyer's right to pass unfavorable criticism of a purchased novel, I do not thereby yield up my own right to criticize the criticism, and I mean the layman's criticism. The paid book critic is another matter. At the moment I want to discuss the unpaid, unpublished critic, the reader.

The purchase of a novel is also in effect the purchase of the right to criticize, but it is far from being a transaction that qualifies the purchaser to speak with any authority. If you don't mind my returning to the earlier analogy, when a man bought a Pierce-Arrow a driver's license didn't come with it. The stupidest criticism that can be made of any novel, or short story, or play, or poem, is when the reader declares he didn't like the subject matter or didn't like the characters, the people. Instead of quoting examples out of other authors' experience I am perfectly willing to give you one from my own. At the end of the year 1949 Miss Dorothy Kilgallen, like many other columnists at the end of the year, made up a list of superlatives. Among her personal nominations was: "Least Worthwhile Woman in Fiction: Grace Tate in *A Rage to Live*." I have a pretty good memory, but that one would have stayed with me anyway, not only because it inevitably conjured up a sort of documentary of Dorothy going through the many, many books she sounds as though she reads every year, but going through them for *not very* worthwhile women of fiction until she found the *least* worthwhile. Assuming that she was conscientious, it must have meant an awful lot of dreary rereading. But aside from the lady's literary chore, as I imagined it, it was noteworthy as an example of a kind of criticism that I can only deplore. I wish there were something else I could do, but deplore is the most I can do. We who write novels are fortunate that in our time there is likely to be a friendlier and wider reception for our best and truest efforts than was the case when as good a man as William Dean Howells was writing. And even later than Howells, much later. I am a new member of the Counsel of the Authors Guild, and I am going to suggest—knowing full well that I'll be wasting my time—that among all the memorials and plaques and awards and trophies, there might be one in memory of Jim Walker, yes, the former New York Mayor James J. Walker, who in the New York State Assembly once killed a so-called Clean Books Bill by remarking that no girl was ever ruined by a book. That immediately brings up the subject of censorship, but let's table that for the moment. I want to register an author's objection to the layman's objection to the author's choice of subject matter and people.

A man, or more likely, a woman who is fresh from the reading of a modern novel will say—and often say it to me—"But those awful people!" In that single comment, whether it's directed at me or at Faulkner or Steinbeck or whoever, the woman brushes off not only the immediate cause of her objection; she also thereby obliterates almost the entire literature of the world since man began to write. I know, because I have tried, that it would be a waste of breath to try to get her to consider the murderers and adulterers and liars and perverts and traitors in what is called classical literature. It would be frivolous to say that the blank verse form has obscured for her the meanings of what she has read, but would it be a form of counter-snobbism to charge her with believing that anything is all right if it was written long enough ago? Not too long ago, in the *Life* before Luce, which sometimes seems almost as

charming as life after death—I once read a bit of criticism
that went something like this: I don't want to see a play
that is about people I wouldn't have to my house for
dinner. The only legitimate reason for the layman's criticism of characters in a novel is the failure of the author to
make the characters credible. It is not now, it never has
been the serious author's job to make his characters nice.
The author who does make his characters nice is a hack
and a liar. He is a hack in the sense that he is writing nice
people for those moments when we only feel like reading
about nice people. If he is reporting, as a novelist, on
characters he has fully understood, but reports incompletely for the sake of niceness or for fear of that awful-
people criticism, he is professionally a liar. And if you
care to search your mental library for authors who fit those
descriptions, you have my freely granted permission to
do so, although the slander and libel laws prohibit my
more hearty cooperation.

It would be easy for me to stand here and say that the
reader has a duty to the author, and so forth. The reader
has no duty to the author whatever. Not even the duty,
which someone more pompous or duty-defining than I
might claim, of finishing a book. Heywood Broun used to
say that he would give any book thirty pages, and I
consider that a fair trial, especially since I am such a slow
reader of fiction and by the time I have read thirty pages I
have pretty well determined for myself how well the author can write. In the relationship between author and
reader the matter of duty is all on one side. The author has
the duty, which is not really so high-sounding as all that
but is really only the job, of writing it the best he knows
how; as honestly and as carefully and vigorously and as
warmly as he can write with whatever he's got. It then
becomes not the duty but the enjoyable task of the reader
to get out of the book all that *he* can, with whatever *he's*
got. If, as we must assume for the moment, he is reading a

book that was written by a man who is out of the hack class, and does finish the book, he has my permission to criticize it on many grounds: he can quarrel with, let us say, decisions that the characters have been forced by the author to make; he can find fault with the accuracy of description and topical matters; he can doubt the trueness of the dialog; he may even have the special knowledge that gives him the privilege of criticizing such technical factors as construction. But if the people have been honestly and credibly made, the reader cannot judge the book or the author for their morals or manners. The reader who does so criticize can more profitably, and really more pleasurably, turn on the television and laugh himself silly. I'm not at all sure, though, that he and I would laugh at the same things, or for the same reasons.

I am not even going to go so far as to say that what this country needs is intelligent readers. I have written four novels that have been what you might call, or I might call, best sellers of the first class, by which I only mean books that have been Number 1 or 2 nationally and for a fair length of time. I also have had three or four other books that got on the best-seller lists just long enough to make their quick disappearances seem like acts of vandalism. This bit of bragging, for which I have asked nobody's permission, serves the useful purpose of backing up my claim to some experience with the novel-reading public. Not all of it has been milk and honey, and I am now not only referring to the problem of taxation, which remains a problem after all the jokes have been made about it. When a novel has reached a sale of 100,000 I can be sure of several results: Bennett Cerf, my wealthy publisher, is going to give me a silver cigarette-box commemorating the event. I have two of those boxes, very handsome, and some day they may be all my eleven-year-old daughter will have to show her children as proof of what a big wheel Grandpa was. I can also be sure that there is no serious danger that I shall establish a racing stable with the money I cling to. And I am equally certain that I am going to spend a lot of time wondering about a country that I happen to love deeply, but that has 170,000,000 people, 38,000,000 television sets, and best-selling novels that get to be best sellers on less than 50,000 sales.

Actually it takes an even smaller sale than 50,000 to get a book on the best-seller lists. Perhaps you might like to hear a small trade secret: an author, his agent, or his publisher, who wants to get a book on a national best-seller list for the purpose of stimulating a movie sale can get his book on the list by buying a few hundred books at certain carefully selected bookstores. He avoids the big stores in the largest cities, but a sale of ten books in one week at a smaller store makes his book a best seller in that store. So he chooses half-a-dozen such stores, and those stores report his book as a best seller. So, as I say, it isn't even necessary to sell 50,000 to have the layman believe that your author friend is now in the market for a cabin cruiser and a Picasso. There is no SEC in the book trade, and the best-seller lists are somewhat less accurate than the quotation listings of the stock exchange. There are, then, best sellers, and there are books on the best-seller lists. I have had both, although I hasten to add that I've never bought my own book to make it look big.

But suppose a novel does get to the 100,000 mark. It's a big figure in the book trade, but in relation to the population of the country, in relation to the number of owners of television sets, or even in relation to the number of Americans who buy Benson Ford's Continental, a $10,000 car, it's dismayingly small. It's less than the circulation of a daily newspaper in a medium-sized city, it's less than a quarter of the circulation of the *New Yorker* magazine, which I pick because *New Yorker* readers are supposed to be the class of the mass. (*Harper's Bazaar, Town & Country*, and *Vogue* don't even run book reviews.) It is less than

the population of Waterloo, Iowa, or Durham, North
Carolina, and, I am told, about one-tenth the population
of this very town. But what is most dismaying is that a
100,000-sale novel has been sold, or must be presumed to
have been sold, to *all*, *all* of the most intelligent readers of
novels. With a smaller-sale novel, say, 25,000—which is a
successful book, by the way—it may be that some of the
most intelligent readers haven't read the book. But with a
100,000 novel you have saturated the potential market, as
the merchandising boys would say. And that, my friends,
is in a time of prosperity. With a sale of 100,000 books you
have reached the limit of sales to the most intelligent
readers, and you have begun to sell to the others. It is no
use to say that the most intelligent readers don't necessarily read the best sellers. They do. Remember now I am
discussing novels, and using the terms novel and book
interchangeably. I am not talking about the technical,
political, economic, soul-searching books of nonfiction. I
am only talking about novels, and when you hear a man,
or woman, loftily say that he doesn't read best sellers, he
probably is not much of a reader of non-best sellers either.
He is, in fact, a bit of a phony, since our outstanding
authors, even Faulkner, always make the best-seller lists,
and the man who declares he refuses to read a best-selling
novel is admitting that he isn't reading our outstanding
authors. So the hell with him. Or her. But when you
consider that you have reached all the most intelligent
readers inside a sale of 100,000 you begin to wonder. You
do if you're an author.

First of all, it is, or should be a great deterrent to the
temptation to let the head swell. A prominent author is
more likely to get a good table at "21" than a good actor or
a government official below cabinet rank, but that's because the people who own "21" have always had an
affinity for writers, and vice versa. But this is not an
author-conscious country. The lower-middle-class French-

man who has opinions on André Gide has no opposite number in the United States. But neither has the middle-middle-class Englishman who has opinions on Graham Greene. It is my glum guess that we now have reached the highest rating we are ever likely to reach in this country, and by "we," of course, I mean the authors of novels. And when you recall a few of the simple statistics I have given you, our highest rating turns out to be dismally low.

Quickly you ask, do you mean the novel is through? Just as quickly I answer, no. Not yet, and not in the lifetime of the children of the youngest person in this room. But I do believe that when the sale of the novel, which after all is a reflection of public interest in it, begins to fall off again as it did in the early thirties and again about five years ago—when that happens again, the novel will not come back.

Why do I make this pessimistic guess? Well, the novel has been in a precarious position all along. The sale of pianos in Grandfather's day didn't help it; the phonograph in my youth and the radio as I grew older didn't do it any good. The tendency among the optimists is to say that the novel has survived the piano and the phonograph and the radio. And it has. But while surviving it was also losing out to the piano, the phonograph, and the radio. Without those various boxes there would have been more readers of novels, and the novel has remained because the population has increased. But there's never been anything like this newest box. It is standard equipment in the American home, and because of it the novel's present top level is the highest it will ever be again. With the best intentions in the world, you still do not curl up with a good book, or a bad book. And most of your children, who are being brought up in the presence of the box, are never going to be readers of novels.

I said the novel has been in a precarious position all

along. The proof of how precarious is oddly enough to be found in the best, that is to say, the most cheerful figures on the novel. Taking a legitimate 100,000 sale, you come down to the maximum number of persons who really care about the novel and you discover that in the United States there are not enough of them to fill Griffith Stadium. I am neither impressed nor encouraged by figures that show how many millions of copies of novels were sold last year. I think we are all too easily influenced by, if I may coin a word, millionship. Millionship didn't do *Collier's* any good, millionship is what the television shows are after—but when they get it the shows don't always stay on the air. I *am* impressed by the dollarship of book sales, but with a big reservation. I would like to know how many of those dollars were spent by people in their late teens and twenties, the people who are going to, or are not going to buy novels ten years from now. I live in a university town, have lived in it for eight years, or two full four-year cycles. I don't see or hear much at Princeton that gives me reason for a rosy view of the future of the novel. And I defy any Yale man to prove there is more culture at New Haven.

I should be able to follow up sour observations with some hopeful suggestions to make for a sweet future. But there are not even enough would-be authors to take the axe to those 38,000,000 TV sets. The Authors Guild has no trained men to sabotage the broadcasting apparatus. And even being in Washington does not make me feel that I am any closer to getting an anti-TV law passed. I'm afraid the best we can do is hold our own, and discourage our children from the novelist's career. By the time that we are able to go around the globe at its fattest in ten hours there may occur a slight national pause for the pleasures of nostalgia or the novel of protest. And there may be enough novelty value in the holding and reading of a book to make one sell like a Presley record, but the present of the novel is more within my sphere and more to my liking than its future. I therefore leave the future and return to the present.

So far I have alienated that section of the novel-reading public that has the impertinence to be critical of the novelist for his choice of material. Then I have gone on to announce that the novel is on the way out. If there is anyone who has a bus to catch, please don't miss it in the hope that in the time remaining to me I am going to turn into Jolly John, dispenser of sweetness and light. This is the part that could be subheaded, "O'Hara Lashes out at Critics."

I am frightfully aware that it is almost impossible for an author to attempt to reply to his critics without seeming like a sorehead or becoming a bore. I confess that when one of my contemporaries, even among those I admire the most, writes a piece or tells the reporters or says in a lecture like this that he doesn't like what the critics say about him—my impulse is to say, "Come on, boy, you've had it pretty good. What are you beefing about?" I know that most of the time the author is justified, and that the critics are wrong. But it just works out that way. When a man has written a novel or a play the reception committee consists of the critics, the professional ones. If they don't like what the author has done, they say so, and for the public that ends it. The public is not really interested in the author's problem, and therefore is impatient with his reply. The nonwriter does not really care how much or how long the author has worked on his book or his drama, and the public consequently is not even interested in the merits of the dispute. The public's attitude is that the author has had his chance, and if he hasn't been able to win the critics' approval, that's too bad, but too bad only for about five minutes, if that. The public in effect tells the author to shut up and go hide, and go back to work on something else. If the author persists, he does seem like a sorehead, and he does become a bore. And I'm very much afraid that almost always I react as the public does.

Now I was not required to take a Consistency Oath before mounting this platform, so I am going to utter a few syllables on the subject of criticism. (The sibilance of the last sentence is accidental, by the way; I am not subtly hissing the critics.) If I end up seeming like a sorehead, it may be that I am a sorehead. A critic—a critic, mind you—recently called me the happy warrior of American letters, and I can't tell you how pleased I was by that, and I don't *want* to be known as a sorehead. But if I am one, it may be because I have been clouted on the skull so many times. If I am also a bore, I can't even beg your forgiveness, and that's the greater risk I run by saying anything at all about critics.

But instead of the more or less routine complaints against critics with which we are all familiar—that they can't write, that they are frustrated authors, that they are jealous, and, in several cases, parasites—I would like to get through this lecture with a minimum of reference to their personal failings and keep the discussion on a higher plane. Not too high, mind you, but on the impersonal plateau. Actually my two last novels have fared better critically than some of my earlier ones, possibly because there isn't very much left to say about me in a hostile way, and also possibly because some critics have finally realized that I am going to go right on writing in spite of their stern refusal to grant permission. After all, that works two ways, too, as I shall illustrate with one personal observation: Twenty-two years ago I was enjoying the success of my first novel, which got good, although not universally good, reviews, and sold well. One day I was reading O. O. McIntyre's column and I came upon a most complimentary mention of me. Do you think I was pleased? I was not. I was embarrassed, and I hoped that no one whose opinion I valued would also see the item. I wanted praise, but I didn't want it from O. O. McIntyre. However, two novels later he made me feel better about the whole thing when he said, and I quote from memory: "Some of the literati say John O'Hara's *Butterfield 8* is swell. I say it's swill." The score was exactly evened so far as McIntyre was concerned, but in my own opinion I gained the advantage. So praise is not all we want. We want it from acceptable sources.

But I know of a quick way to bore you and that is to tell you some of the nice things that have been said about me. I want to get on to the other stuff. The first thing an author is entitled to in a review by a professional critic is accuracy. Some of you who are keen students of the American novel must recall that I got some pretty bad reviews on *A Rage to Live*. Almost all of the unfavorable criticism was directed against (a) the social system of a small American city, and (b) the morals of the principal female character, Grace Caldwell Tate. Now I have often been accused of an overwhelming preoccupation with the American social system, and I intend to say something about that later. But the men and women who criticized that part of my novel almost invariably stated that I had returned to the Pennsylvania of *Appointment in Samarra*, *The Doctor's Son*, and *The Farmer's Hotel*. *A Rage to Live* was about a different city in a different location, with any number of subtle and obvious differences. But a disturbingly large number of the reviews even went so far as to say that *A Rage to Live* took place in Gibbsville, in spite of the fact that there is a fairly long sequence in the novel devoted to a *visit* to Gibbsville, during which the heroine finds herself in the company of people who are strangers to her. *The Farmer's Hotel* was read by many, many fewer people, but again there was a remarkable number of reviewers who whizzed through that short novel without noticing that it took place in the Pennsylvania Dutch farming country, with no connection with the anthracite coal industry that is so important a part of Gibbsville. Pennsylvania is a large as well as a glorious state, but some of the reviewers, the lazy ones, would have it about the size of Rhode Island. To them I recommend a nice stroll from Chester to Erie, just about this time of year. In the matter of the morals of the leading lady of *A Rage to Live* I suppose I had better choose my words with great delicacy. Especially since there may be listening to me some people who made the same mistake some of the reviewers made. It was frequently reported in reviews that Grace Tate was one of the most promiscuous women in literature. That may be all right as an opinion, but not very good as a statistic. The truth is that in her husband's lifetime Grace Tate was unfaithful with one man. Marital fidelity is praiseworthy and desirable, and one extra-marital love affair constitutes infidelity. But to call Grace Tate promiscuous and to throw stones at her as a chronic adulteress was shockingly bad reporting. In life, in nonliterary living, you would have a hard time making the charge stick even if you included her love affairs after the death of her husband. Please take my word for it that inaccuracies of the kind I have mentioned are far from rare.

I have no doubt that what has been called the explicitness of detail in my novels is partly responsible for the mistakes that some reviewers have made in writing about the emotional life of my characters. Here I am not referring so much to the number of affairs that Grace Tate may or may not have had, but to the attacks on her as a loose woman. An Edith Wharton woman or a Willa Cather woman, or for that matter a Fran Dodsworth, does not get such harsh treatment from the reviewers, but it seems to me that the difference is only in the author's treatment, and *only* in the author's treatment. The significant detail that makes for full character development is not only to be found in the kind of flowers and china and fabrics a woman shows to her friends. The novelist's privilege, and in my opinion his duty, is to tell all he has to, even when it means dispensing with the pretty reticences that his characters may affect or that he himself may have. If a man's entire work is to be judged every time he publishes a book, then judge him by his entire work. Or, if only the immediate book is to be judged, then judge that work. But not many critics are willing to settle for one or the other. They wanted to put Hemingway out of business on account of *Across the River and Into the Trees*, forgetting that *To Have and Have Not* was his least successful novel, while remembering that he had written *From Whom the Bell Tolls*. In other words, practicing an eclecticism that was unfair to the author. Either way has its good points: to review all of an author when his newest novel comes out, or to pretend that his whole career rests on this one new novel and as though he had written no other. But by the same token it is ignorant criticism to base an attack on a whole novel on what is really the reviewer's public distaste for sexual detail. There is no responsible author who gratuitously introduces sex. The author who does so is irresponsible and foolish, since it somehow becomes apparent even to the layman that it has been gratuitous and that the author hasn't much else to offer. The author who writes a novel without introducing sex has automatically limited the extent of his responsibility and is thus not entitled to full artistic consideration. And that's aside from whatever he may be inadvertently revealing about himself.

I am often asked, too often asked, what I think about censorship, and usually by people in and out of the press who don't really care what I have to say about it, just so long as I am against it and offer a quick and easy solution to a problem that has no quick or easy solution. I fancy myself as a liberal, a vanishing phenomenon, and I therefore concede to the Roman Catholic and other churches, the Anti-Defamation League, the Navy League and almost any other organization the right to invoke its own kind of censorship if that censorship is some form of the boycott. I do not recognize the right of any organization to practice censorship at the source, which is, first of all, the author, and secondly, the publisher. I have no idea—and apparently neither has anyone else—how to construct federal or state legislation that will permit freedom of political and artistic expression and at the same time restrict the publication and sale of the smut magazines at the candy store. I think we are overlegislated as it is, and not only in the book world, and I think it is also time for me to say thank you and let you go home. Thank you, and goodnight.

8 ✒ We All Know How Good We Are

The first author to receive the Academy of Arts and Letters Award of Merit for the novel was Theodore Dreiser, an author with whom I have much in common. The second was Thomas Mann, whose work I admired. The third was Ernest Hemingway, who was a friend of mine and, as some of you may recall, the author of a book which I reviewed favorably, and in so doing may have set back the cause of favorable reviews a couple of decades. The fourth author to get this award was Aldous Huxley, whom I admired chiefly for his erudition. I am honored indeed to make that quartet a quintette, to find myself in

John O'Hara was awarded the Merit Medal for the Novel by the American Academy of Arts and Letters and the National Institute of Arts and Letters on 29 February 1964. His acceptance speech was published in facsimile as a Keepsake for the O'Hara Memorial Exhibit at the Pennsylvania State University Libraries in 1970 and is published here through the courtesy of the Pennsylvania State University Libraries. The title has been supplied by the editor.

such company, and I trust they are not made uncomfortable by my presence, even at this distance.

But it is really not the company that I have been placed in that is the source of my pleasure today. Rather it is the company of men and women who have accorded me this recognition. Baseball players cherish the M.V.P.—Most Valuable Player—award because it is given them by other baseball players. The baseball writers, in other words, the critics, are the ones who decide on the elections to the baseball Hall of Fame, but the players themselves vote for the M.V.P. award, and they really know. The men and women of the Academy give of their own prestige, since they have all been recognized and honored before they are elected to the Academy. This, then, is unquestionably the highest recognition, the top honor I have received in my professional career, which began forty years ago when I entered the newspaper business, and began again thirty years ago when I published my first novel.

Thirty years is the length of time that the anthropologists and the sociologists call a generation, and the coincidence that I am a whole generation removed from my first novel is a significant one. Today my first novel is studied in prep school English classes; when it came out, I was reviled and my book was banned. At least *some* of the liberties that the younger writers enjoy today were paid for by me, in vilification of my work and abuse of my personal character. That is one of the things I have in common with Dreiser and, to a lesser extent, with Hemingway. The public library that kept *Jennie Gerhardt* in the cellar— which is where I first read it—also kept *Appointment in Samarra* in the same cellar, in 1934. But don't think that that was peculiarly a small-town judgment. Go back, if you will, and read Sinclair Lewis on the subject of *Appointment in Samarra* and me, as of 1934, in what was then known as the *Saturday Review of Literature*. These obvious facts need restating today because in the context of present-day writing I am regarded as obsolescent, and rightly so. I continue to experiment in every story and in every novel that I write, but the experimentation is in techniques rather than in point of view or in principles. There are things that I am for and things I am against, and they have not changed much in thirty years nor are they likely to. The fully rounded irony is that I can expect the same degree of abuse from the new critics for my 1964 conservatism that I got from my critics for my lack of restraint in 1934. But as long as I live, or at least as long as I am able to write, I will go to the typewriter with love of my work and at least a faint hope that once in a great while something like today will happen to me again. We all know how good we are, but it's nice to hear it from someone else.

I thank you.

9 ✄ Every Great Writer of Fiction Was a Great Social Historian

In spite of the fact that it is almost thirty years since I first came to London, and in spite of the fact that London is one of my favorite cities, this is my debut as a public speaker in your town. On my earliest visits, while I was still a young man, I gave what might be called a series of private lectures in such cultural institutions as the Ivy restaurant, the Savoy Grill, the 400 Club, Quaglino's, l'Apéritif, the Savage Club, and various locals in S.W.3.

John O'Hara spoke at a Foyles Bookstore luncheon marking the paperback publication of *The Lockwood Concern* in London, 3 May 1967. Copyright © 1972 by United States Trust Company of New York, as Executor of and Trustee under the will of John O'Hara. Reprinted from *John O'Hara: A Checklist*, edited by Matthew J. Bruccoli, by permission of Random House, Inc. The title has been supplied by the editor.

My comments on your manners and customs were not always well received. Perhaps I was overconscientious in my endeavors to be fair. That is to say, to be just as fair to the English as countless Englishmen since Mr. Dickens had been to my country. As you know, Mr. Dickens and many other gentlemen, less talented but equally observant, did not fail to notice certain imperfections in my homeland. I therefore took it upon myself to achieve a fair balance. But there is no such thing as a fair balance in matters of this kind, and thirty years ago no one remembered that Dickens and all the others had had their say about the United States. Consequently my informal lectures in the Savoy Grill and the 400 Club were treated with disdain, as though they were the intemperate utterances of a youngish man who had a great deal to learn about England and as much to learn about his capacity for whiskey.

Regrettably I have learned the hard way that my capacity for whiskey is nil. Rather less regrettably I have learned a little more about England. Or let me say, immodestly, that I have learned a little more about the human race, in which I gladly include the English.

Whether I like it or not—and sometimes I don't—I have been tagged with the epithet, social historian. When it is used in complimentary fashion, the label is a dangerous one because an author so described may begin to think of himself as a social historian and fall into the habit of writing like one. It is probably safe to say that every writer of fiction was a social historian. We can go further and suggest that every great writer of fiction was a great social historian. But he was first of all and always an artist, and what more could he ask? I don't know the origin of the term, but I am inclined to suspect that it was invented by a critic who believed that it was more profoundly complimentary to call an author a social historian than an artist. At the risk of being judged unfair—a risk I am

willing to take in the case of critics—I shall go on suspect-
ing that it was a critic who decided that Dickens or Zola or
Balzac could be made to seem more important by calling
them social historians. Since I want you to feel that I am an
important *something*, and as I am much too modest to
insist that I am an important artist, I address you today as
a social historian. You should get home in time for tea,
stimulated to the point of exhaustion by the things I have
told you. If tea does not revive you, I urge you to knock
back a few whiskies, and I wish I could join you.

As a social historian it becomes my duty to give you hell
for the things that have been happening in your country,
and you are supposed to sit here and politely take it. But
I don't see how I can give you hell without—in all
fairness—placing some of the blame on my own country.
As a matter of fact, many of the things that I don't like
about England today are un-English, and when I come
here from time to time and find so much that is un-
English, I am bitterly disappointed. Some of you may
have seen what has happened to Times Square, in New
York City, and to Forty-second Street. The honky-tonk
atmosphere has taken the place of the old-time glamor,
and while there is plenty of excitement in that area, it is
the kind of excitement that makes me stay away from our
Broadway and hasten to the peace and quiet of yours. As I
have said on other occasions, when the English copy the
Americans they copy the wrong things. I was distressed
some years ago to discover that the works of Damon
Runyon were enjoying a vogue in England, and that there
was a cult of Runyonados who affected Runyonesque
speech in the entirely erroneous belief that there were
people who talked that way. The thing I most disliked
about Runyon's writing was its fundamental dishonesty.
I knew Runyon and I knew the people he had in mind
when he was writing. They were no damn good. They
were thieves and chislers, and if any of them had had a

heart of gold it would have been cut out of them by their companions. The sad thing is that Runyon could have been a social historian; no one knew the gangsters·and the gamblers and the pimps and prostitutes better than he, and he could write. But he never told the truth about them. He gave them a sort of raffish innocence that made them as acceptable as the characters in P. G. Wodehouse. Come to think of it, Wodehouse invented one Runyonesque character. I refer to the pig, but it was a well-bred pig.

I suppose that there have been thousands of Americans who lived and died without ever knowing that the English countryside was not inhabited by murderers and murder victims. You must realize that the only English books many of my countrymen have read were mystery novels, and that a rather gory picture was presented of the goings-on in the stately homes. The hacks who wrote your mystery novels were as much to blame for this somewhat inaccurate picture of rural England as Runyon for his picture of urban America, but possibly because Runyon wrote more effectively he did the greater harm. At least I never heard of an American cult that tried to talk like Lord Peter Wimsey. We do have in the United States an organization called the Baker Street Irregulars, who put on deerstalkers and read self-consciously scholarly papers on the works of Sir Arthur Conan Doyle, but Sir Arthur is entitled to serious consideration as artist and social historian, if only because he can transport you back to the England of his time, the sights and sounds and smells of London and the countryside, so economically and so truly. The plots of Sir Arthur's stories are wasted on me; I read and reread them to spend a few hours in a place and a time that existed before I was born. It is a time and a place that I sometimes wish I could return to. Failing that, I come to the United Kingdom once in a while and try to ignore what I do not wish to see. You will agree, however, that it becomes increasingly difficult to avoid the sight of the strange young creatures who call attention to themselves with their odd attire, while at the same time hiding their identity behind growths of hair. This, by the way, is one of the mysteries of present-day youth, this business of dressing eccentrically to achieve distinction, and at the same time encouraging a hirsute bush that automatically robs them of recognition. It is true that Lady Godiva covered as much as she could with her long tresses, but today's young people are hardly motivated by the same high principles. It occurs to me that if Lady Godiva were to ride bareback in the Haymarket at noon tomorrow, she would be safe from the peeping Toms. The peeping Toms can now sit comfortably in a striptease joint in no danger from Lady Godiva's charger. In our country we have been having a vogue of restaurants with topless waitresses. Over here I suppose they would be known as milk bars.

Enough of that. I am more or less at peace with the Lord Chamberlain at the moment, and I'd like to keep it that way.

When I was invited to make an appearance here, it was suggested to Mr. Graham Watson, who so capably handles my literary affairs in the U. K., that my discourse might be on the subject of literary awards and their effect on authors. I have been wondering about that. Mr. Watson also represents Mr. John Steinbeck, and I suspect that someone must be under the impression that all of Mr. Watson's clients are winners of the Nobel Prize. Not so. I confess that there was a time when I thought I had a chance of going to Stockholm to get the medal and the 15,000 guineas or whatever it is in cash. I even practiced saying "Thank You" in Swedish. "Tack så mycket," one says, and they reply, "Var so god." It was not just an idle dream. A renowned winner of the Nobel who lived in London passed the word on to an English friend of mine that I had been up three times or maybe it was four. I was so sure that my turn would come that I promised myself a

Rolls-Royce if I won. Well, I have the Rolls-Royce, but I gave it to myself as a consolation prize two years ago when it became certain that the Swedes were not even going to give me a Volvo.

I have grown so fond of my Rolls that if the Swedish Academy were to offer me the Nobel, conditionally on my giving up my Rolls, I would be compelled to say, "Tack så mycket, but no, tacks." An author with such a frivolous attitude is probably not Nobel Prize material anyway. Hemingway never bought a Rolls. Faulkner never bought a Rolls. Pearl S. Buck never bought a Rolls. Sinclair Lewis never bought a Rolls. Steinbeck never bought a Rolls. Tom Eliot never bought a Rolls. And I would hazard a guess that none of those rather obscure authors whom the Swedish Academy likes to surprise us with will be found on the rolls of Rolls-Owners. You must, you *must* be serious. You must be deadly serious, as deadly serious, let us say, as dynamite. If you are likewise obscure, in both meanings of the word, it is so much the better. The somewhat less than unanimous approval of the award to Steinbeck was caused, I believe, by the fact that whatever else he may or may not be, Steinbeck is not obscure. At the time of the award to Steinbeck one critic complained that Steinbeck and I were lightweights. Immediately the question arises, "Then what is a heavyweight?" I suggest that the answer to that is to be found in the unreadability of so many writers who never learned what writing is for. Writing is for reading, as music is for hearing, and painting is for seeing. Writing for reading is an even more serious obligation to its creator than music for hearing is to the composer or painting for seeing is to the artist. Music, of course, has an advantage that writing and painting lack. Strike a C-chord and you get the attention of every man, woman, or child, regardless of their intellectual capacity. A painting, a drawing, has an almost equally elemental, fundamental appeal. But the art of writing presupposes the existence of a reader with a trained mind, trained at least to the degree that the printed words will have meaning. You and I do not open a volume in Sanskrit or Japanese or even the Cyrillic and make any sense out of the characters. It is usually forgotten, in highbrow discussions of the various arts, that writing is the only art that demands special training on the part of everyone who takes even the slightest interest in the form. H. L. Mencken once declared that no one can appreciate music who has not learned to read the bass clef. I disagree. No one loves music more than I do, and I have long since forgotten how to read the bass clef. I listen to some music every day of my life. As for the graphic arts, all you need is an eye or two. You look, you are attracted or repelled or both. But to appreciate writing you first have had to learn to read.

Now of course I am not going to argue that the woman who reads every word of *News of the World* is more of an intellectual than the woman who reads nothing at all but spends her leisure hours in the Albert Hall or the British Museum. But let us strike a medium. As Noel Coward did not say in *Blithe Spirit*, some mediums should be struck regularly, like gongs. Let us invent an average person, let us call her Mrs. Tommy Atkins. Let us say that our Mrs. Atkins is an educated person, educated up to the university level. A literate person. Able to read. And let us say that our Mrs. Atkins does read, not only the *News of the World*, but occasionally the novels of Mr. John Braine, Mr. Graham Greene, Mr. John Steinbeck, and other authors who have taken pains to be readable. I mention only a few, but a noteworthy few of the authors who, different though they may be, one from another, do have in common this conscientious approach to their work. Our Mrs. Atkins may turn away from one of these authors because she does not care for his people, or because she does not care to be preached to, however, subtly. But she does not turn away because of these authors' unreadability. I cannot make that point too often. I make it as often as I can because the intellectual community, the highbrow critics, have got into the habit of dismissing readability as a small virtue and very nearly a fault. It is not hard to see why. I read these critics and they are unreadable in 700 words, but that does not keep them from being disrespectful to a novel of 700 pages. By the way, you must not expect modesty from me. I am just as aware as anyone else that my books have sold something like 15 million copies, and I could not have attained that circulation if I had not been readable. Dear Mrs. Atkins, may her tribe increase. Since 1934 I have published more than twenty-five books—novels, novellas, and collections of short stories. One of the very nicest things about you English is your loyalty to your entertainers, your actors and actresses and variety artists. To some extent this devotion is matched by your willingness to do the same for authors. But Mrs. Atkins does not go on reading an author who ceases to be readable, and for this no one is to blame but the author. Let an author become careless or cocky or simply written out, and Mrs. Atkins will abandon him. I am very happy to say that she has not abandoned me. After thirty-three years, beginning with a best seller, and often in spite of Mr. Connolly's enemies of promise, I still manage to find my books on the current best-seller lists. And do you know why? Because I give them what *I* want. Not what *they* want. The author who believes he is going to *give them what they want* is making a great, great mistake, for the truth is that they don't know what they want. And for an author to attempt to anticipate what they want is an act of dishonesty. It may be all very well for a Gracie Fields to come out once again and once again to sing the "Biggest Aspidistra in the World," and for Louis Armstrong to sing "Hello, Dolly!" for the ten thousandth time. But the casualty list of authors who repeated themselves is long and dismal. They paid for their dishonesty with the loss of Mrs. Atkins's loyalty.

We're getting somewhere. I am sneaking up on a point, and that point is that the authors who love their work and are conscientious about it are the first to know when carelessness or cockiness or creative sterility sets in. The distractions and diversions can be temporary or totally destructive, and they can be anything from booze to women to greed to too much praise. Between the invasion of Poland and the Japanese surrender I found that I could not write anything longer than a short story. You might say that it took a world war to keep me away from my typewriter. You might also say that when I got back to my typewriter I went to work with a vengeance—a vengeance, possibly, on those critics who said I was written out. Well, the revenge has been sweet, not because I have demolished my critics, but because I have been doing what I want to do and to my satisfaction doing it better than I had ever done it before.

In one sense I could call myself a war profiteer—in the sense that I profited by the long absence from the typewriter, during which I built up a reserve of impatience and frustration that finally, when I got back to the typewriter, converted itself into energy. If you are the sort of egocentric, sensitive individual who chooses writing for his lifework, wartime is an emotional experience like no other. No one escapes the dreariness and the drama, and when you have been previously conditioned by your work to see and hear and share every detail of human behavior, there is not a single minute that does not provide you with—and here comes that awful word—material. At such a time you are rather like a man locked inside the Bank of England, surrounded by cash but unable to spend a penny. But when the opportunity came, when peace of a sort was restored in the world and I no longer felt that it was my duty to second-guess the Prime

Minister and the President of the United States, I found that my resources were practically unlimited. I am not exaggerating when I say that I could keep busy for the next ten years. I know, for instance, what my publishing schedule will be in 1969. The one thing I dislike about getting older is that it is no longer physically possible for me to stay at the typewriter for seven or eight hours at a stretch, which I have been known to do many times. After four hours at my desk I find that when I try to raise my 14 stone deadweight, my legs buckle under me. If that were not so, I could predict with accuracy how many books I shall have published between now and 1975, when I hope to have the original Mrs. Atkins's grandaughter among my readers.

I touch upon the physical resources only lightly, since it is perfectly obvious that after sixty we can all expect to slow down a bit, and I am sixty-two. Last year I had to become reconciled to the fact that even such an undemanding pastime as golf was taking it out of me. My physician told me that I ought to take more exercise, but my surgeon told me that my bad back was inoperable. I had been playing golf for almost fifty years, and I could have won the British Open IF I had only worked as hard on my golf as I do on my writing. The same with tennis. You'd have seen me out there on the center court at Wimbledon, saying, "Hello, Queen," but for the fact that when I was four years old I learned to read. By the way, it was around that time that I first contracted a mild case of Anglophilia which has been with me all my life. An aunt of mine—an American, of course—used to give me every Christmas a copy of THIS YEAR'S BOOK FOR BOYS. She was not of Irish descent, and I sometimes wonder why she chose that Edwardian volume of insidious British propaganda. But I loved it, although I never was won over to cricket. However, I was never really won over to baseball either. Reading, and then writing, never had to win me over. I took to reading, and writing, as the child Mozart took to music. When I was about six someone gave me a hand-printing set, and I had my introduction to moveable type. While most normal, healthy extroverts were out robbing birds' nests and setting fire to small buildings, I was setting type, copying the headlines in the newspapers and so on. I was not very gregarious at that age. Instead of team sports, I went in for solitary riding. I had a horse before I had a pony. If there was a note of pious disapproval in my reference to boys who robbed birds' nests, I hasten to disavow it. I didn't steal the eggs from the nests—I shot the birds. Also, my need for companionship was satisfied at home, since I was the first-born of a brood of six sons and two daughters, and whether you pronounce it privvacy or pryvacy, it's a rare treat in a family so large. My father was a surgeon, and presumably knew what caused babies, but it didn't seem to make much difference. In New York, by the way, there is a young and pretty actress who has six children, and when someone said to her that she must be either a Catholic or a sex maniac, she replied that she was both. Like my father.

I, by the way, have one daughter. Her husband is an officer in the Navy and she lives on the Island of Guam. They have been married since last September, mind you, and I am not yet a grandfather. I present this vital statistic to show that not all the young people today are in as much of a hurry as we sometimes believe. Not even the United States Navy.

Did you want me to come here today and inflict upon you a quarter of an hour of esoteric dissertation on the art of writing? As I turn into the homestretch it occurs to me that the general tone of my remarks has been, to say the least, informal and nonintellectual, and that one or two of you may feel that you have not been given your money's worth. If that is the case, I'm sorry. As they say in the

courts, I plead guilty with an explanation. As I said a
while ago, this is my debut as a public speaker in your
country—and very likely to be my farewell appearance as
well. I never make speeches at home, or give interviews or
appear on the radio or the TV. I am doing it now because
my friends at Hodder & Stoughton and the New English
Library are very persuasive, and they are convinced—
without quite convincing me—that an author's personal
appearance does a lot to help sell his books. I was strongly
tempted to point out that my books have been selling very
well in the United Kingdom without benefit of personal
appearances to stimulate the sales. I could still argue the
point. But I will admit that I could not think of a better
excuse for coming to London, and I am very fond of
London. Indeed, my favorite cities in the world are London and Edinburgh, and if I had to live in a city—which
thank God I don't—I would settle for, and in, either one.
Therefore it is no great hardship to make the journey.
However, I know that I am a terrible public speaker, and
when I have listened to myself on tape recordings I am
appalled by the gruff sound of my voice and my Pennsylvania twang. Even if my father had sent me to
Stoneyhurst and Oxford I'd probably still speak the way I
do, which is all right at home, where we have had to listen
to Wendell L. Willkie and Lyndon B. Johnson, but not all
right for an English audience accustomed to the mellifluous Olivier, the clipped Coward, and the plastic accents of
the B.B.C. With that handicap in mind I had to try to
overcome the disadvantage of *how* I was going to speak by
what I had to say.

Well, I could be literary, or literahry. I could offer you a
quarter of an hour of literary comments and observations
so profound that they could be embalmed in the *Times
Literary Supplement*. Or, I could be controversial, by saying disrespectful things about Mr. Toynbee and Sir
Charles Snow, among others. Now I have never been one

to avoid controversy, literary or otherwise. I have been mentioned in certain dispatches for my recklessness in that regard, and for an essentially peace-loving man I seem to have attracted more than my share of hostility, and expect that I shall continue to do so till my dying day. There are a few scores to settle with the Englishmen who come to the United States (many of them, I regret to say, giving every appearance of taking up permanent residence) and tell us what's wrong with us. You have exported some beauties that you must have been glad to get rid of, if only temporarily. But there is a time and a place for everything, as my grandmother used to say, and as I am sure your grandmother used to say. Maybe your grandmother said it first. In any event, I decided that this event was not the one at which to hold forth on literary technology or Mr. Toynbee or the situation in Rhodesia or the offensiveness of some of your expatriates. I could touch on all these matters in a way that would give you a strong hint as to what I believe, and yet manage to avoid putting you to sleep or giving you apoplexy. This, after all, is our first meeting, and if it also turns out to be our last, I still want to feel that the decision not to return was mine and completely unofficial. I have had only the slightest acquaintance with Mr. George Raft, and that in Hollywood thirty years ago.

And so my decision was to prepare a lecture, if you can call it that, which would repay you for the courtesy—and the curiosity—of coming to break bread with me. As Mr. Pepys would say, I did on my good suit, I scraped my face, and here I am, shirking my duty as a visiting American author by not pointing out the things that you should change. My American publisher sometimes declares that I have mellowed. Maybe so. If you are mellow, you do not bellow, and I may have done enough bellowing thirty years ago, in my lectures at the 400 Club and the Savoy Grill, to last me a lifetime. Today, not chronologically today but at this stage of my life, I am too full of admiration for the English people to make sensational criticisms for the sake of sensationalism. I am perfectly content to be what I am, a middle-class American, impulsively chauvinistic, and more than satisfied with what happened in 1776. But because I am a middle-class American, and sixty-two years old, I do not feel that I lose face by publicly acknowledging our debt to the English middle class. From you we acquired a sense of decency and fair play, respect for the rule of law, and standards of conduct that add up to civilized behavior. We inherited these virtues and we do not always follow the rules or meet the standards, and neither do you. But they came from you. Britain is the home of the middle class, and in the middle class resides middle thinking and middle behavior, the kind of middle thinking that you return to after too much hope, too much despair, too much action to the right and too much action to the left, too much abandonment of the good and decent things that belonged to the past—for God knows none of us can say what good and decent things belong to the future, or if they do. I am not here to seek to change anything, if change means—as it does—to steer you away from one course into another. That would be the sort of impudence that I deplore in some of your intellectual exports to my country. But I cannot in conscience pass up this opportunity, in this one little minute, to try to restimulate your pride in yourselves and in what your ancestors gave to the world, the strong self-respect that enabled you to respect one another, by habit if not by instinct to respect each other's small rights—as in good manners—and thus to respect each other's larger rights, as demonstrated by observance of the rule of law and the implicit right to change the law, any law.

I am going home the day after tomorrow, to go back to work as a social historian. Thank you.

Unpublished Essays and Forewords

10 ✍ These Stories Were Part of Me

The selection of these stories became easy the minute I stopped making it difficult. I have had, besides one volume of Pal Joey pieces, 129 short stories published in my own collections (*The Doctor's Son and Other Stories*, *Files on Parade*, *Pipe Night*, and *Hellbox*). Every one of those stories has been mentioned by some critic or other, so if I were to go on critical mention I would have to reprint the whole 129 now. Or, if I were to go on what friends have said, I would here and there have to include a story only because of one line of dialog or one descriptive passage, which happened to be favorites of those friends. There was also some talk with the publishers about making the selections on a geographical basis, or chronologically. But I could not please everybody, so I decided to please only myself.

I went through the stories and quickly wrote down the titles of the stories that I liked best, in some cases not even rereading the stories. When I came to the end of the list I had thirty-one stories of varying lengths, of differing times, and of scattered locations. They are, I think, my best.

Most of them were written in the twenty years from 1930 to 1950, during which I believe I wrote more short stories for the *New Yorker* than any other author. Aloofness is not one of my characteristics, so I cannot pretend that I have not been grievously hurt by the magazine, which in commenting on my stories was pleased to call

Previously unpublished. Written as the foreword for *Selected Short Stories of John O'Hara* (New York: Modern Library, 1956), but not used. The typescript is in the Estate of John O'Hara. The title has been supplied by the editor.

121

me "the master" but in reviewing my novels was perfectly willing to make fun of me and even to distort what I said by the cheap trick of quoting out of context. The high principles that they peddle in "Notes and Comment" don't even last till the back of the book. Well, damn their eyes.

I don't think I'll write any more short stories. In very recent years I have been made sharply aware of the passage of time and the preciousness of it, and there are so many big things I want to do. But during the thirties and the forties these stories were part of me as I was part of those nights and days, when time was cheap and everlasting and one could say it all in 2,000 words.

J. O'H.

Princeton, New Jersey
November 1955

11 ❧ I Was Determined to Make Plain What I Had Seen

One of the New York newspapers—the *Sunday Daily News*—carries a feature that fascinates me. It shows a photograph of a New York street scene today, and another photograph of the same scene forty or fifty years ago. The camera angle is the same in both pictures, and I imagine they try to approximate in the modern photograph the time of day and season of the year when the earlier photograph was taken. I suppose the quick appeal of this fea-

Previously unpublished. Written as the foreword for a new printing of the Modern Library *Butterfield 8*, but not used. The typescript is in the Estate of John O'Hara. The title has been supplied by the editor.

ture is that the horse-drawn vehicles and the streetcars and the early automobiles, and the clothes and moustaches of the human beings of the earlier time, are so different from the vehicular and pedestrian traffic of today, and therefore funny. But to me the remarkable thing is that so many of the old buildings are still standing. Fifth Avenue has changed completely, north of Thirty-fourth Street; Park Avenue is now changing for the second time, from private residence to apartment house to office building. But elsewhere on Manhattan is amazingly unchanged, regardless of renovations and false fronts.

I used to come to New York once a year when I was a small boy. I would be taken to the show at the Hippodrome, and annually I would go back to Pennsylvania with some new theory as to how the bathing girls in the Dillingham spectacles would descend into the onstage swimming pool and never again be seen. (Now that I think of it, I still don't know what happened to them; I met Charles Dillingham in later years, but I forgot to ask him what the trick was.) But the big treat for me was not the Hippodrome, nor the hot fudge sundaes at Huyler's, nor the peppermints at Maillard's. My special pleasure was the ride on the bus, up Fifth Avenue and then over to Riverside Drive. The buses always went too fast for me. There were plenty of Pierce-Arrows and Packards and Locomobiles in my hometown, and the chauffeurs wore breeches and black leather puttees; but in Pottsville, Pa., nobody had a town car and nobody had a chauffeur and footman on the box. There was only one Rolls-Royce (which incidentally was owned by a rich bachelor who also kept a Rolls in New York). On the ride up Fifth Avenue I would see Hispano-Suizas and Isotta-Fraschinis and Minervas and Daimlers, and Hudsons and Cadillacs and Roamers and Stearns-Knights and Lelands and Cunninghams and Danielses and Templars and Marmons with bodies by Brewster and Schuette and Derham and

Fleetwood and Amesbury. On the bridle path on River-side Drive I would see some fine saddle horses with beautiful tack and properly turned out riders. From the top of the bus I would often see footmen in knee breeches opening the front doors of the Fifth Avenue mansions. All this was a better show than Harry Houdini and Annette Kellerman and the Six Brown Brothers (without Harriman) at the Hippodrome. I was curious about those town car-and-footman people, but only moderately envious; I somehow took for granted that when I got big I'd have all that too. This was not even a dream or a hope. I just took it for granted, as I took it for granted that when we went to Philadelphia, we stopped at the Bellevue. That was our hotel. In many ways I was a practical boy, in that I always found out how much a thing would cost; but I must have been ten years old before I fully understood that my father's patients paid him money to operate on them, or that the people who worked for my family as servants were rewarded with cash. It never occurred to me that Maggie Ward and Arthur Woodward and Nat Bohler were being *paid*, and it is therefore not so strange that I *assumed* that I would have money and the getting of it presented no problem. I was about fifteen years old before I heard anything about the income tax, and what I heard was my father raising holy hell because he had to pay $1,500 that year.

So my approach to New York was conditioned very early by a fantastic ignorance of money matters, so that when I finally did get there, to work and live, and in spite of the fact that my father had died just about broke—my attitude was that of defenseless optimism. New York would take care of the newcomer. Well, New York did, but not in my optimistic use of the phrase. Within two years I was literally starving, by which I mean that for one three-day stretch I went without anything to eat. The experiences of those first two years did not make a banker of me, and they were not all as disillusioning or as difficult as those three days. But you never quite get over the degrading, debasing experience of going hungry (Henry R. Luce chose that particular moment to dun me for $50 I owed him). You learn to see things very plain, and not only things but people, and not only people but a city. Six years after I arrived in New York I was the author of a highly successful first novel and was already at work on *Butterfield 8*, in which I was determined to make plain what I had seen.

I was, of course, helped by fact. This is my only *roman à clef*, taken, as it was, from the headlines of a newspaper story, plus a great deal of digging, plus a slight personal acquaintance with the pathetic girl whom I call Gloria Wandrous. The book was a shocker to the literary cocktail party set that I have never had any part of, and who have written me off almost annually for the past twenty-six years. The story of Gloria Wandrous had appeared as fact in the newspapers, along with her excerpted diary that could not all be printed either in a newspaper or a novel. If anything, I toned the story down, and I can be reasonably certain that my novel was read with relief by some clubmen and litterateurs who were mentioned in the original diary. The novel was not highly regarded artistically, and the Pulitzer Prize that year went to Josephine W. Johnson for *Now in November*. (The drama prize went to Zoë Akins for *The Old Maid*.)

Now, a quarter century later, I look upon the book as I do one of those old New York buildings that are pictured in the *Sunday News*. The novel is not remarkable for the differences so much as for the similarities to 1930 in 1960. A gentleman whom I shall describe as a noted historian—and he is just that—told me two years ago that *Butterfield 8* is the one novel that historians covering that period must read. When I consider what the Toynbee School feels about mere fact in history, I am inclined to believe that my novels may all be as reliable as the work of the formal historians of our time. Unfortunately we novelists must also strive for readability as well as for verisimilitude. Or is that so unfortunate?

John O'Hara

September 1960
Princeton, New Jersey

12 ✒ Characters in Search

I had to become a writer. My father was a successful small-town doctor who also made a little money, and I was born and brought up a Catholic. My antecedents, even those who came here in the eighteenth century, were practically all Irish except for a few drops of English and German that it is too late for me to do anything about. All my life I have been rebellious. My father and mother were well-educated people, and I am not. Put those items through an International Business Machine and out comes a card marked Writer.

But lately I have been worrying about a serious professional oversight on my part. As a small-town boy who was sent away to (and from) second-rate schools I have come across quite a few Characters in my lifetime, but I haven't done much about them. The hell of it is, except for this piece I don't think I ever will. I just don't seem to be able to handle these people and so since they all appear to me to be too good to waste I offer them to, say, all the pretty little girls who are taking short-story courses at Smith College, and never have read *Winesburg, Ohio*.

Previously unpublished. Published from the undated typescript in the Estate of John O'Hara.

Only two of my relations achieve the list. One was my grandfather. He was six foot four. He was in the Union cavalry and when he came back from the war (including a certain march to the sea) his men gave him a purse of gold. He went on a glorious drunk with the money. While on this drunk—he was wearing his uniform—he pinked a friend with his saber, and when he sobered up and learned what he had done he became a highly unpopular prohibitionist. He made one rather cynical epigram about women and horses, but I still have to save that for personal interviews, which are not to enjoy second-class mail matter privileges. I guess he was fairly stock and pretty dull, really, so I'll get on to my great-aunt.

Auntie was on the other side of the family. She was something like one hundred and three when she died, still unmarried. Although she was born in Ireland she might as well have been born in Scottsboro. All through her life she hated Abraham Lincoln, and on the other hand she nursed Union soldiers. (She was a nurse.) She was a devout Catholic, and all during Prohibition I made a neat profit by providing her with drugstore gin which I sold her at just twice what I paid for it. I loved her and she loved me and I was sorry I did not get to her funeral, which was held from my grandmother's house. Two of my brothers made it, though, and on the morning of the funeral they kept singing "Auntie Doesn't Live Here Any More."

Several of my Characters rate hardly more than a line. King Philip, for instance. King Philip was so-called because he looked like a picture of King Philip in Sadlier's History and was said to be half Indian. I guess he was Italian because he lived in a solid Italian section and he didn't understand English, but when we would yell "King Phil-l-lup-p-p" at him he would chase us. Once he chased us and I fell down a coal chute in Schott's grocery store. (Local joke, by the way: "Hear about the murder at

Second and Mahantongo? . . . George Schott the Corner Grocer.")

Another Italian, considerably younger than King Philip, is included here because whenever we jolly kids saw him we would yell: "Drop that 'n' run!" and whatever he was carrying he would drop, and he would run. I'm afraid he is on my conscience, like a boy who was in my Sunday School class. When Miss Rinehart, our teacher, wasn't looking we would form a sort of scissors with our fingers and whisper to Schwartzie: "Gonna cut your ears off, Schwartzie. Gonna cut your ears off," and he would dash out of the church.

Eggy the Boy Engineer was usually good for a chase. He was a rather grimy man who wore the best clothes in town—after they had been worn by their original owners. He was a part-time gardener for some of our leading families and he was always attired by Brooks, Langrock, Bell, Macdonald & Campbell or better. All you had to do was call to him, "Eggy the Boy Engineer," and he went after you. He was fleet of foot and when he caught you he would give you a good root in the tail.

Dory Sands was a fat little man who was having an honorable career as street cleaner until he was persuaded to run for public office. He considered standing for mayor but compromised by putting on an interesting campaign for Council. As a reporter I would interview Dory every day and every night. He had political cards printed by the thousands and as was customary among candidates, he sent half barrels of beer to the fire companies. He quit his job on the broom and I was very sorry to see him lose. He went into a decline after the snub by the electorate.

Dory had been quite well known before he went into politics. His name and Jack Kantner's were scrawled on walls in the public and parochial schools and all saloons. Jack was remarkable chiefly for his nose, which made Durante's seem retroussé, and for his grin. I was fond of

Jack and we had a kind of understanding. When he was not in jail, which was known as Stoney Lonesome and Hotel Kantner, he would hang around my father's office until he saw the old gent come out. My father was a fanatical dry, but he was a soft touch for lushes. Jack would tell Dr. O'Hara that he was cured of the drink and wanted five bucks to make himself presentable so he could get a job. The same night Jack and I would buy each other at least one drink out of respect for the source of our funds.

Three of my characters deserve mention only for their names. One was a Pennsylvania Dutchman, who spoke scarcely a word of English. He was always turning up in some farmer's barn in our valley. He was a Civil War veteran and was known only as Unie. Another man, a young gangster, who because of his complexion was called Screendoor—like looking at him through one. The third was just a fat little tart whom nobody gave a tumble in my prep school days. She called herself Dardanella.

I never actually got to know the Dombrowskie family for the same reason that I was fascinated by them. They lived on the edge of town and they had a large collection of fine, healthy rattlers and copperheads.

The most inveterate first-nighter of our town was a bit more complicated than the others. He was in his seat every Monday and Thursday when the vaudeville bill would change. We called him Violets. One night when we were sitting in a car and gave him a more or less per-functory salute he came over to the car and said: "You better thtop calling me that," and pulled out, enough for us to see, a Colt's .45 automatic. We were more careful after that. He used the gun on himself when they caught up with him at the factory where he was a bookkeeper.

There was nothing complicated about the last man on my list. He told them all to go to hell. He had a good business and he worked hard six days of the week. The seventh he would spend at a place which was known by courtesy as a roadhouse, which all the nice people had to pass on their way to the country club. And he did it right. He parked his car where everybody could see it, and it was the snappiest, yellowest, most expensive roadster in town. He was all boy.

Well, that's thirteen off my chest.

13 ◣ My Favorite Room

My favorite room is the one in which I now sit and compose this paper. It took me a long time to get this room the way I want it to be, and if I did not like it I would have only myself to blame. A few professional interior decorators and some semipro amateurs have had a look at what I have accomplished, and the politest compliment I have been given was from a professional who gave the room and its contents a full, silent, two-minute inspection and said, "Well, its *you*."

When we were building our house I asked for control of only two rooms: my study, and my bath, and I got it. I like a small bathroom, and mine is the size of an A-Deck bathroom in the Queen Mary. There I robbed myself: the tub is not long enough for me to stretch out in. However, it is deep enough for me to get a good soak and probably safer than a long tub would be. I usually work late into the night and then take a warm bath before going to bed, and if I had a long tub I might possibly fall asleep and drown. A man in my hometown drowned in the bathtub, and I

Previously unpublished. Published from the undated typescript in the Estate of John O'Hara, this essay was written after "Linebrook," the O'Haras' Princeton home, was built in 1957. The essay continues with reminiscences about Hollywood actresses, which have been omitted here. The title has been supplied by the editor.

still remember, as his epitaph, the drearily repetitious
jokes about his dying a clean death. In fact all I remember
about Mr. Halberstadt is that he had two attractive
daughters, Mary and Imogene; that he drove a Maxwell;
and that he died in the tub. I do remember that the
Halberstadts had a big tree in front of their house, in the
center of the sidewalk, and you had to walk around it. I
happen to be a great lover of trees and I wish to give the
Halberstadts full credit for not disturbing their tree,
which I think was a horse chestnut, but I am not able to
say whether it was Mr. Halberstadt or his wife who was
the dendrophile. Now that I have thought it over and
taken myself back fifty years, I incline to the belief that the
tree was an oak. If there is anyone who lived in the 1600
block on Mahantongo Street, Pottsville, Pa., and remem-
bers the tree in front of the Halberstadts', I would be glad
to hear from him, or her. The Halberstadt girls were like
Norma and Constance Talmadge, in that Nim Hal was,
like Norma, the prettier, but Mary Hal, like Constance,
was the cuter. There was always a bunch of girls on their
porch: Elizabeth Fox, Peggy Mould, Margaretta Arch-
bald, Sara Shay, Lucetta Ibach. If there had been a Junior
League in Pottsville, they would have been it. In any
event, I got my small bathroom.

On F. Scott Fitzgerald

14 ✒ In Memory of Scott Fitzgerald: Certain Aspects

It is granted that Scott Fitzgerald was not a lovable man, but most of the time he was a friendly one, and that characteristic, in a man of his professional standing, is as much as anyone can ask. I always warmed to Scott, was always glad to see him, always. But then if you saw him too long a time his intelligence, about which he was almost overconscientious, would go to work, and he would let you bore him. He would almost encourage you to bore him. He let you go right ahead, being banal and uninteresting, and knowing how much you were embarrassed yourself by your ordinariness. At the same time he was professionally one of the most generous artists I've ever known. Dorothy Parker pointed that out to me one time when I had some reason to be irritated with Scott, and though Dorothy Parker has said many true things, she has said nothing truer than that. I guess the loneliness of his private hells was so enormous that he really would have got no great relief by sharing a little of it, in other words by letting you know him better, and so he figured to keep it all for himself. Well, that was his business and thus he kept his integrity, which I won't attempt to define, simply because everyone who knew him knew he had it.

And he kept it in death. I read the *Herald Tribune* obit, and I understand the *Times* one was just as bad. The curious hostility of those pieces may be attributed to that

John O'Hara wrote this reminiscence of Fitzgerald for a symposium in *The New Republic* (104 [3 March 1941], 311) that included contributions by John Dos Passos, Budd Schulberg, John Peale Bishop, Malcolm Cowley, and Glenway Wescott.

integrity coming through even to people who didn't know Scott, who probably hadn't even read him. (I am reliably informed that the piece in *Time* was written by a man who until he was assigned to do the piece never had read anything of Scott's). The integrity, the aloofness, came through and annoyed some people, and so they just went ahead and wrote their angry little pieces, saving their wit and tolerance for some spectacular Bowery bum or deputy chief inspector of police.

F. Scott Fitzgerald was a *right* writer, and it's going to be a damned shame if the generation after mine (I am thirty-six) and the one after that don't get to know him. I had the good luck to read *This Side of Paradise* when it first came out, twenty years ago, and I've read it practically annually since then. He was the first novelist to make me say, "Hot dog! Some writer, I'll say." I was younger than his people in *This Side of Paradise*, but I was precocious. Amory Blaine's mother's maiden name was Beatrice O'Hara, and I was in love with a girl named Beatrice then, a coincidence that became less important page by page. The people were right, the talk was right, the clothes, the cars were real, and the mysticism was a kind of challenge. By the time *The Beautiful and Damned* and *The Great Gastsy* appeared, the man could do no wrong. In a burst of enthusiasm I once said to Dorothy Parker, "This guy just can't write a bad piece." And again she was right. She said: "No. He can write a bad piece, but he can't write badly." He sent me the page proofs of *Tender Is the Night*, which was a major honor in my life. I read it three times then, but only twice since, for that fine book is not to be read just any time. It's a dangerous book to encounter during some of the moods that come over you after you're thirty. You don't like to think of yourself, lone, wandering and lost, like Richard Diver, going from town to town in bleak upstate New York, with All That behind you.

And then a year ago Scott invited us out to his house in

the San Fernando Valley for Sunday lunch. It was going to be a big thing, though a small party. He was going to have Norma Shearer and Loretta Young, and I wish I had told him that if I were choosing people to lunch with I would not pick either Norma Shearer and/or Loretta Young. Anyway, they weren't there. There were only my wife and I. The food was good and there was a lot to drink, but I was on the wagon and Scott was not. He was terribly nervous, disappearing for five and ten minutes at a time, once to get a plaid tie to give my wife because she was wearing a Glen plaid suit. Once to get a volume of Thackeray because I'd never read Thackeray, another time to get some tome about Julius Caesar which he assured me was scholarly but readable—but which he knew I would never read. Then we went out and took some pictures, and when we finished that he suddenly said, "Would you like to read what I've written, but first promise you won't tell anyone about it. Don't tell them anything. Don't tell them what it's about, or anything about the people. I'd like it better if you didn't even tell anyone I'm writing another novel." So we went back to the house and I read what he had written. He saw that I was comfortable, with pillows, cigarettes, ashtrays, a coke. And sat there tortured, trying to be casual, but unhappy because he did not know that my dead pan was partly due to my being an extremely slow reader of good writing, and partly because this *was* such good writing that I was reading. When I had read it I said, "Scott, don't take any more movie jobs till you've finished this. You work so slowly and this is so good, you've got to finish it. It's real Fitzgerald." Then, of course, he became blasphemous and abusive, and asked me if I wanted to fight. I saw him a few times after that day, and once when I asked him how the book was coming he only said, "You've kept your promise? You haven't spoken to anyone about it?"

15 ✒ Scott Fitzgerald— Odds and Ends

One day about a year before he died Scott Fitzgerald invited my wife and me to lunch at the place where he was staying, the guesthouse on a movie actor's ranch in the San Fernando Valley. He wanted that lunch to be something a little special because a few weeks before he had disappointed us at the very last minute by telling us at 8 P. M. that he simply could not appear at a dinner party which we had built around him and some New York friends of his. He simply could not face that many—thirteen—people. That left thirteen at table and an extra girl, and I was pretty sore. But as always happened, with me and with everyone else who had the same admiration and affection for Scott, I got over it. After the initial invitation to lunch he called us several times again; he said he was thinking of asking L——, a beautiful movie actress. Did we know her? Like her? Well, we knew her, and didn't like her, but we didn't say so. Next day he called and said he had decided not to ask L—— and was asking N——, also a beautiful movie actress. Actually he never invited either charmer, but he was glamorizing our lunch in advance. He wanted it to be something special, and it was.

When we rang the doorbell the door suddenly swung open and there was a little man in a rather startling Halloween mask, muttering Gullah or double-talk. We took it big and Scott enjoyed that. We sat down to lunch very late because we did a lot of talking, or at least Scott did. At that precise second in history both he and I were on the wagon, but I guess both of us were showing off

Review-article about Edmund Wilson's edition of *The Crack-Up* (New York: New Directions, 1945), *The New York Times Book Review* (8 July 1945), 3. —"Scott Fitzgerald—Odds and Ends" by John O'Hara © 1945 by The New York Times Company. Reprinted by permission.

before my wife and we were talking about writing. After lunch he went upstairs and got some books (a life of Caesar and something of Thackeray's) for me, and a Glen plaid tie for my wife, which exactly matched her suit. Then we were back at writing-talk, and as I say, this day was something special because Scott brought out his notebooks containing the kind of random, fugitive memoranda that many writers keep, and then he made me comfortable with cushions, cigarettes, cokes, and asked me to read what he had written on *The Last Tycoon*. I had no way of knowing that the stuff Scott was showing me that afternoon was to provide at least a parttime career for one of our most distinguished critics, but of course I have no way of looking into the future, and you never can tell about critics.

The critic in this case is Edmund Wilson, who already has shall we say sponsored the unfinished *The Last Tycoon*, and who now appears with a book which bears the title *The Crack-up*, by F. Scott Fitzgerald. Edited by Edmund Wilson. It also has on the title page these words: "With Other Uncollected Pieces, Note-Books and Unpublished Letters—Together with Letters to Fitzgerald from Gertrude Stein, Edith Wharton, T. S. Eliot, Thomas Wolfe and John Dos Passos—And Essays and Poems by Paul Rosenfeld, Glenway Wescott, John Dos Passos, John Peale Bishop and Edmund Wilson." The book is published by New Directions and retails at $3.50.

Fitzgerald at least once called Mr. Wilson his "intellectual conscience" and because of that I find myself wondering where was Wilson's own intellectual conscience when he "did" this book, for I regard its publication as an unfriendly act. Let us examine the contents of the book in the order of their appearance:

Item: a piece called "Echoes of the Jazz Age." This came out in, I believe, the old *Scribner's* in 1931. It was a fast and accurate report and restatement of the period to which

America gave Fitzgerald's name. Item: "My Lost City," a kind of sequel to the other, which Fitzgerald handed to his agent in July, 1932. Item: "Ring," which was Fitzgerald's contribution to the stockpile of Lardner obituaries, and the best of that lot. It contains the sentence: "He had agreed with himself to speak only a small portion of his mind." This one appeared in 1933, and in the twelve succeeding years and in all the years preceding Lardner's death no one has spoken wiser literary words about Ring. Item: a piece called "Show Mr. and Mrs. F. to Number——." Hotels he had stopped at. Item: "Auction—Model 1934." Junk he had bought. Item: "Sleeping and Waking." Sleeping and waking. Item: "The Crack-up." The orgy of self-pity which, characteristically, the magazine *Esquire* and the critic Edmund Wilson thought was good, but which should have been suppressed at the mailbox. ". . . And if you throw me a bone with enough meat on it I may even lick your hand." Item: "Early Success." What every young writer should— and does—know.

Those items, even when they are bad, are the only legitimate excuses for the trouble, if any, Scott Fitzgerald's Intellectual Conscience went to. . . . At least they are Scott Fitzgerald, signed by him and therefore by him approved for publication. That's the chance you take when you put a piece in the mail; you take the chance of its being published, forever somewhere in print to be exhumed by a candidate for a Master's Degree at Hardin-Simmons College or by a critic who was your friend and is your literary executor.

Then on, relentlessly, to the notebooks and to the letters from Fitzgerald to (naturally) Edmund Wilson and others, including Fitzgerald's daughter, and to Fitzgerald, mostly from established writers to whom Scott had sent what must have been extravagantly inscribed copies of his books. The To-Fitzgerald letters we can pass up without further comment, but the notebooks and the From-Fitzgerald letters, or their publication, demand our belligerent if brief attention.

F. Scott Fitzgerald was the author of *This Side of Paradise*, *The Beautiful and Damned*, *The Great Gatsby* and *Tender Is the Night*, among other books. Each, of course, was good, and they were all different, but any man (or woman) with the slightest feeling for fine, truly fine, writing must see that all of Scott's writings had this one thing in common: they were the work of a most conscientious craftsman. That isn't good enough, really. He was a tortured, experimenting, honest artist. The stuff read so easily that perhaps you had to have some feeling for writing and perhaps the tiniest curiosity about it to be aware of the conscientiousness of it, the sweat and tears and, literally, in Scott's case, the blood. I once said to Dorothy Parker, "Scott can't write a bad piece."

"You're wrong," she said. "He can write a bad piece, but he can't write badly."

And, of course, as usual she was right. But we were speaking of *Tender Is the Night*, which we had just read in page proof. We were speaking of a work that had been completed and approved, which had taken five years and more in the doing. We were not speaking of notebooks and letters which never had been intended for publication.

Great writers' letters (and, I suppose, their notebooks) often are interesting. They have an attraction for the busybody in all of us, and to my way of thinking a small case can be made out for their private publication. It is possible that this book may easily achieve the status of private publication, but I doubt that that was Wilson's intention, and unless it was his intention he has done Fitzgerald a disservice in throwing together this collection of odds and ends. You don't do that to a painstaking artist. Or maybe you do, if you are a critic.

There is a good deal of cop's blood in an individual who makes a career of being a critic, and while the policeman's lot is said not to be a happy one, my sympathies are understandably and always with the poor slob who gets it with a nightstick.

On Aug. 15, 1920, in a letter to Wilson Scott Fitzgerald said: "For God's sake Bunny write a novel and don't waste your time editing collections. It'll get to be a habit."

That's all, brother.

16 🖂 An Artist Is His Own Fault

A little matter of twenty-five years ago I, along with half a million other men and women between fifteen and thirty, fell in love with a book. It was the real thing, that love. As one who tries to avoid the use of simile and metaphor, I cannot refrain here from comparing my first and subsequent meetings with that book to a first and subsequent meeting with The Girl. You meet a certain girl and you say to yourself, in the words of a 1928 song, "How long has this been going on?" The charm has to be there from the very beginning, but then you see that this time it is more than charm (although charm can be enough). The construction, of book or girl, has to be there from the very beginning, but then you see that this time it is more than the construction (although construction can be enough in the case of the girl). Well, not to hack away at the point too long or often, I took the book to bed with me, and I still do, which is more than I can say of any girl I knew in 1920.

After the appearance of that book I was excitedly interested in almost anything that was written by F. Scott

Introduction from the *Portable F. Scott Fitzgerald*, selected by Dorothy Parker. Copyright © 1945 by Viking Press, Inc. Reprinted by permission of The Viking Press. The title has been supplied by the editor.

Fitzgerald; his novels, short stories, and his nonfiction articles. He was born in September 1896 and I got here in January 1905, both of us just for the ride, but in spite of the at that time very important difference in our ages I regarded him as one of us. He knew what we were talking about and thinking about, if you could call it thinking, and what he knew was every bit as true of us who were of Earth '05 as of the '96 codgers.

The novel was *This Side of Paradise*. It is not included in this volume. Mrs. Parker did not consult me in making her selections for this volume, and it is only my job to write an introduction. I have no quarrel with her selections, either. Get that straight. Within the limitations of space she has brought together a truly representative collection, and please bear in mind not only that these words of mine are an introduction to this book, but that this book itself will turn out to be an introduction: an introduction to Scott Fitzgerald for the pleasure of those who haven't had the pleasure. This may not have been the publishers' or Mrs. Parker's intention, but I am fairly certain that it's going to work out that way.

Cantering along on that assumption, we can take first things first, and so, in book-jacket language, a word about the author. He would have been fifty next year, but if ever a man was not meant to be fifty, it was Fitzgerald. I don't mean that he tried as hard as Ernest Hemingway not to be fifty. Most of his life Ernest Hemingway has followed the big shooting as doggedly as Mr. Morgan used to go after the Scottish grouse, whereas Fitzgerald never heard a military shot fired in anger. Fitzgerald in his way, though, did go into battle, and when you read about the beating of Dick Diver by the Italian Fascist bums in *Tender Is the Night* you will see what I mean. Scott was ever one to like thinking of himself as a man of action and I commit no libel when I say he could be quarrelsome. The last time I talked to him he telephoned me—we were both in Cali-

fornia—to ask me to serve as his second in a duel. A
Hollywood trade paper had blasted a girl whom
Fitzgerald admired. He wanted to fight a duel with the
editor of the paper, and it seemed to me that if Scott won a
duel with that editor he would be doing no disservice to
the Hollywood community, but, stalling for time, I
pointed out that under the code duello, as I understood it,
the challenged and not the challenger had the choice of
weapons. "I'm sure he's no better with foils or sabers than
you are," I said, "but he may be a damn sight better shot."

"I didn't say anything about shooting," said Scott. "I'm
just going in his office and beat the hell out of him, and I
want you to come along so the rest of his bastards don't
jump me."

I had a type-louse's-eye view of the the two of us going
to that print shop, pushing past the receptionist, and
Scott taking the editor apart, which I honestly think he
could have done. The two men were about the same
weight and height, Scott was a bit younger than the
editor, and he had Righteous Wrath and a Lady's Kerchief
on his side. But I couldn't see the editor's goons standing
idly by during this performance, and I couldn't see myself
doing a William Farnum to a succession of Tom Santschis.
Hot lead can be almost as effective coming from a linotype
as from a firearm. I therefore attempted Reason. I told
Scott that it was a laudable enterprise he had in mind, but
pointed out to him that he would be doing the lady no
good, that he was a married man with a daughter in
college in the East, and that if he went storming into a
"newspaper" office and we had a brawl in defense of a
lady's honor we would just make the first pages of the
early editions of practically every afternoon paper in the
land—not to mention the Paris edition of the *New York
Herald Tribune* and *Time* magazine. The notoriety would
be notoriety and nothing else; if you kill a cop, all cops
hate you; if you thrash a newspaperman all newspaper-

men except his immediate competitors hate you, and the stories that would appear would not be very understanding about his defense of the young lady in question.

"In other words, you're saying no," said Fitzgerald.

"If you insist on going, I'll go with you, but I don't want you to go and I don't want to go with you."

"That's all I wanted to know," he said. "I thought you were my one real friend in this town. I'll get Eddie———. He's diabetic and he doesn't get into fights, but he's a gentleman."

He hung up.

He was telephoning from a place where he had to call through the operator, so I immediately dialed Eddie, who was a friend of mine, and told him what to expect. The strange thing was that Scott did not telephone Eddie, who sat in his room all morning preparing arguments against Scott's project. Maybe Scott realized that what I said made sense; he surely knew instinctively without my telling him; and maybe he was actually counting on me as a friend to talk him out of the assault and battery (with intent to kill). Who knows? But I do know this much: although that was spring and Scott didn't die until December, he never telephoned me again.

The above sad little anecdote could be matched or bettered by any of the men and women whom Scott knew and loved best: Dorothy Parker, Robert Benchley, Maxwell Perkins, Charles MacArthur, Hemingway, Gerald and Sara Murphy, Edith Wharton, Edmund Wilson, John Dos Passos, Ring Lardner, and Harold Ober; the Princeton pals whom he would suddenly remember after ten or twenty years and even boys who had gone to Newman, the lace-curtain Catholic prep school which he attended; the beauty and talent of Hollywood in the twenties; the beauty and talent and corruption of the Riviera in the twenties and thirties; the favorite barkeeps everywhere; the Curb & Snaffle set in Maryland and Long Island; the casual pick-ups between Santa Barbara and St. Jean de Luz whom Scott would invest with something or other they didn't quite have, but who for a while would think they had it—whatever it may have been—all along, and which Scott would let them have whenever he thought of them. He never really lost track of anybody. The first man I ever met who knew Scott Fitzgerald was a trying snob who had been in Scott's class at Princeton, who came to my dinky hometown for a Winter Assembly because the girl who asked him hadn't been able to sew up the captain of the Yale football team. Ten years later, when I was getting to know Fitzgerald pretty well, I mentioned the fellow. Scott hadn't seen him since my meeting, but Scott knew enough about his marital, social, and economic progress to make you think they were seeing each other all the time. Mind you, Scott didn't like him, never had, and hadn't known him well in college, but it was characteristic of Scott to be a sort of class secretary, except that the class included—at my guess—50,000 men and women. I have a pastime, which is to read *Who's Who*, and I am up on a large number of persons whom I haven't met, don't expect to meet, and don't particularly want to meet. With Scott it was something more; contributing an anecdote or a physical description or some scandal, success, or failure.

This predilection of Scott Fitzgerald's could easily have been confusing to him in his work. I imagine that part of the time he would find himself writing about people he knew, but frequently he must have had the sometimes doubtful pleasure of meeting a person whom he had once created for a story. The one was as real as the other. His work had that all the time: verisimilitude, reality, truth. This was true even when he took exercises in fantasy, a line of endeavor which usually bores me, because I haven't the patience and whatever other equipment is essential to the understanding of symbolism. He always knew what he was writing about, which is so, so untrue of so, so many so-so writers. It may not seem like much in 1945, when it is done all the time, but twenty-five years ago it was delightful to find a writer who would come right out and say Locomobile instead of high-powered motor car, Shanley's instead of gay cabaret, and George, instead of François, the *chasseur* at the Paris Ritz. These touches guaranteed that the writer knew what he was talking about and was not getting his information from Mr. Carnegie's local contribution to culture. The reader usually knew, without stopping to think much about it, that if a family owned a Franklin it was because they didn't feel they could afford a Pierce-Arrow. A prejudice persists among some eye-weary souls who are professional book critics that men's clothes, for instance, are not worthy of description. I can think of one fellow, for instance, who used to earn his living at book criticism but is now a sort of radio announcer, who used to suffer terribly when Brooks Brothers was mentioned. And yet if a writer were to put the fellow into Brooks Brothers clothes you would recognize him right away for a spy. If, as is most unlikely, the same critic knew about guns, I can imagine his shrieks at the luckless, careless writer who would confuse a Webley with a Savage, or if boats were being discussed, let the writer make a mistake about a suit of sail and the whole work would be suspect. And properly. This particular ex-reviewer doesn't, however, know much about clothes, and there are photographs to prove it. Scott Fitzgerald had the correct impressions because, quite apart from his gifts, the impressions were not those of a man who's never been there. As we used to say, he knew the forks.

It is a dangerous thing to bother about the rich. A writer who does it in this country—at least during and since the times when barbers and bootblacks were piling up fabulous fortunes of from five to forty thousand dollars—will find himself regarded as a toy. The professional pipe-smokers—chiefly book critics and editorial writers—could understand *The Great Gatsby* because who couldn't? Too, Fitzgerald put one over in that book; he made the important rich man seem like an unimportant heel, and Gatsby, a man who happened to have a lot of money but was not a rich man, was made so pitiable that there were those who loved him. In the story frankly called "The Rich Boy" you get a four-reel motion picture of a rich man, in Technicolor, but the pipe-smokers never made much comment on that one, probably because it was a short story and they didn't have the name of O. Henry or Maupassant to identify it. But in two novels which dealt with the rich, Fitzgerald gave them, the rich, the business, yet the choice of those novels appearing in this volume was snooted by the conservative press no less than by the liberal and leftist. I was annoyed, but I don't recall having been surprised. In this country the rich don't write; there are really so few of them, and they can't write anyway. Americans who write, and those who write criticism almost without exception are of middle-class origin no matter whom they write for or what they write, the *Wall Street Journal* or the *Daily Worker*. They have very little contact with the rich or none at all. The exceptions are the small number of men who get to know the rich at Yale, Harvard, or Princeton. Nowhere else. The rich don't go to other colleges. The rich I mean are the kind of people who can say, "If you have to ask how much a yacht will cost, you can't afford it." You give a thought to how few men get to know the rich in college, and how few of *them* become writers, and you will see why there is very little accurate writing about the rich, and you will see why there are no critical standards for dealing with the rich, and why the public will just as readily accept, oh, say, Louis Bromfield or Edna Ferber as it will Scott Fitzgerald. About the public I am not really complaining. An artist is his own fault. But a critic who passes judgment on a novel by Frederick Prokosch or the Shangri-La book—or for that matter, a novel about sharecroppers—ought to be curious and careful and conscientious enough to be something besides casually contemptuous of a work of art. To wit: *Tender Is the Night*.

But Scott wasn't only a man who better than anyone else wrote about the rich. Actually most of his work was about the middle class, your family and mine. And in this book there is a short story called "Absolution" which shows he left the Plaza Hotel on occasion.

Yes, he had a place in American Literature. Scott Fitzgerald had a place in American Literature. Somewhere between Arthur Dwight Croveney and the Deep Blue Sea? All he was was our best novelist, one of our best novella-ists, and one of our finest writers of short stories. The dynamite money goes to other authors, one of whom I am sure was given her cheque for $46,000 and her Chinese visa with all the unlimited grace at Fitzgerald's command. To a now rather grumpy playwright went another 46 G's for his somewhat less than indigenous observation of the American scene. To a third American author, the same sum, complete with medal, for his capable christening of a character who culturally set us back a fast fifty years, because a lot of people were satisfied to be that character. Possibly it is not gracious of us Americans to refrain from establishing a ten-million-dollar fund to pass judgment on Swedish letters, Swedish being just as tough as American. And yet you look in an old *World Almanac* and reexamine the awards handed out by the trustees of Columbia University and it might strike you that Gothenburg—the one that is not in Nebraska—is at least as close to home as is Morningside Heights. Gothenburg and Morningside have in common no mention of F. Scott Fitzgerald.

The custom, which I intend to follow, is to compare the

artist with his contemporaries. Hemingway was more of a contemporary of Fitzgerald's than Sinclair Lewis. Still, Lewis and Fitzgerald were writing about the same times, while Hemingway, good and influential as he was, wasn't using the same material. Fitzgerald and Lewis were covering the same ground at the important time, but it's funny to read the two men on the same subject. Lewis, then, and Lewis right this minute, is King of the Corn—and by way of being the Sweetheart of it. The names that Lewis dreams up are as improbable as those you will find in *The Chronicles of Clovis* or *The Unbearable Bassington*. Lewis now is accepted as a satirist when it can be devoutly doubted that he was trying to be anything but a commenter on the American scene. It always has seemed to me that one day Lewis woke up to find himself called a satirist, and became one by continuing to play straight. Fitzgerald was no satirist. Not even in *The Great Gatsby*. If he was being a satirist, as has been claimed, I don't get it, and I am no dope. He burlesques—not too broadly, since it wasn't necessary—the squandering of money on Long Island in Prohibition days, it's a fact he did. That wasn't being satirical; that was only a slight heightening for the ultimate effect of showing for all time one very sad man who was, except for his love and death, an ass, and I wish I could go further and tell you what animal I am thinking of. (You put a saddle on the animal.) No, my friend, Fitzgerald had more than satire to offer. The satire was implicit for all to see, just as a writer's politics are there for anyone to see who has the curiosity and intelligence to wonder. Politically, Scott was an anarchist, as is anyone who is not a fascist or a religious Communist. He never said he was cynical of all the governments and all the governing; it was just there to be seen. He never wore a badge saying, "Tee-hee, I'm a satirist."

I speak of Sinclair Lewis, who, of course, is Johnny One-Note. This fact remains a 33rd degree secret from the

Nobel and Pulitzer judges, who patiently regard the American male as something between Will Rogers and the roles best played by Walter Huston. Come down heavy on your r's, don't dress Eastern, be a tall-size hypocrite, and your creator automatically wins half the heavyweight prize. Remember, too, if you are the author, that the female sex is to be handled in pasture, once over lightly. Any other treatment just shows how you stand on the question of virility. Fitzgerald didn't feel that way, act that way, or write that way. Fitzgerald could believe that an American man and woman were capable of married love, and that if a husband heard the call of the wild it wasn't inevitably toward the direction of a plump, inexperienced organist or a plump, bored woman in a hotel with a funny quasi-Indian name. For a man who has always been around and who periodically takes an austerely moral stand (curiously reminiscent of Rollin Kirby's Prohibition cartoons), Sinclair Lewis has some strange ideas about the sack-time of American men. On the subject of extralegal love you will come across two sentences by Fitzgerald the like of which are not available in any Lewis that I recall. They read: "For a long time afterward Anson believed that a protective God sometimes interfered in human affairs. But Dolly Karger, lying awake and staring at the ceiling, never again believed in anything at all." Even without reading the story ("The Rich Boy") is there anything wrong or much lacking in that? Not to be too rough on Lewis, give him his due: he can write about bank buildings and receptacles for used razor blades and he can almost approximate the speech of an unwitty Abe Martin and he can make you remember that George F. Babbitt's middle initial stood for Follinsbee, but he hasn't put down a man or a woman who is the real thing. God knows I have encountered thousands of Babbitts, but I don't believe in Sinclair's particular George.

Who else is there who might be considered a professional contemporary of Fitzgerald's? Hemingway I will
not discuss while there is a war on, for he writes best
between wars and I think his best work already is familiar
to many readers to whom this book really will be a
Fitzgerald introduction. Who else? I honestly don't think
of anyone else. The collegiate material was handled by
Cyril Hume and Cornell Woolrich and Katharine Brush
and Percy Marks and Stephen Vincent Benét and Lynn
and Lois Montross, but who among the new Fitzgerald
audience would know whether Benét wrote *The Wife of
the Centaur* or *The Beginning of Wisdom*? There is even a
strong possibility that only Benét's name among them
would have a familiar sound. If I were to get on the
squawk box and say to Fighting 18: "Now hear this: Carl
Van Vechten is aboard and will be pleased to answer any
questions"—would the fighter pilots know what the hell
to ask him? I hardly think so, but when you have read this
book you might care to know that Van Vechten's slim
volumes (*The Blind Bow Boy*, *The Tattooed Countess*, *Nigger
Heaven*) had a little of the same screwy life that was caught
by Fitzgerald in *The Great Gatsby*. A minor but sharp
talent called Jack Thomas produced a pleasant little item
called *Dry Martini*, but I myself haven't read that since
Thomas died, which was almost fifteen years ago. Most
certainly other writers were at their scrivening in the
twenty years of Fitzgerald. The only trouble is I can't think
of them without doing the kind of digging that I am
postponing until I start bucking M.A., which must wait
until I get my bachelor's, which must wait.

Notwithstanding his sure place as an American writer,
it was a happy circumstance that Fitzgerald was not a lit'ry
figure. He was not a literary-tea boy (none of the good
ones are), and moreover his readers, the greater number
of them, were people who could take a book or leave it
alone. He was an artist and at the same time enough of an

artisan to sell stories to *The Saturday Evening Post* and still say what he wanted to say. "Babylon Revisited" appeared in the *Post* while George Horace Lorimer, not exactly an *erotica* man, was boss. Except for a small part of the revelation of the incestuous relationship between Nicole and her father, *Tender Is the Night* was first serialized in the old *Scribner's*. He wrote a lot for the magazines without an ignominious amount of compromise. It goes without saying that all who read him in the *Post* did not buy his books, just as it goes without saying that all who bought his books did not take as gospel or even as ultimate entertainment every word he wrote. But he *was* a *popular* writer. He reached an astonishing number of people who spent not half as much money on books as they did on golf balls or lingerie clasps. Those who were old, and those already committed to being old, never got around to him as they did take to Louis Bromfield, say, who was around Fitzgerald's age and who also was around in Fitzgerald's era. What is to be hoped for with this collection is a new and enormous and appreciative audience not unlike in joy of discovery the Sherlock Holmes fans who came along many years after Doyle had put a stop to Holmes. In my generation (I am forty) and among men and women now in their fifties can right now be found a good-sized number who are able to compare notes on Fitzgerald's work without quite going so far as the Holmes fans, who form clubs and go to their meetings by hansom cab and wear deerstalker caps. That is how real Fitzgerald character and incident have become to many of us. I go to the Plaza Hotel two or three times a week, not with any genuine expectation of running into Paula Legendre or Scott Fitzgerald. You will find a few pages on that Paula died in childbirth, and you already know that Scott is dead. And yet, last week, during those exhaustingly hot days, I saw Anson over and over again, sometimes in uniform and sometimes not. And last year I saw a pregnant girl who could have been Paula Legendre. And always, without fail, whether I'm going to the Plaza for a haircut or a drink (or even to talk over the arrangements covering this Introduction) I am half prepared to see Scott himself. He was elusive in life, God knows, and all through the writing of this piece he has refused to stay put, but the ectoplasm or the artist need not bother the reader or even me. For after all the *stuff* is here. The stuff is very much here, and it's mellow.

Long Island, July 23, 1945.

Book Reviews and Reading Lists

17 ✍ Good Reading

John O'Hara, author of *Appointment in Samarra*, recommends the following:

Man's Fate, by André Malraux (Smith & Haas).
Tender Is the Night, by F. Scott Fitzgerald (Scribner's).
A Farewell to Arms, by Ernest Hemingway (Scribner's).
Laments for the Living, by Dorothy Parker (Viking).
The Last Adam, by James Gould Cozzens (Harcourt, Brace).
The Great Gatsby, by F. Scott Fitzgerald (Scribner's).
Good-Bye, Mr. Chips! by James Hilton (Little, Brown).
Round Up, by Ring Lardner (Scribner's).
The Complete Short Stories of Saki (Viking).
The Man Who Knew Coolidge, by Sinclair Lewis (Harcourt, Brace).

"These," Mr. O'Hara concludes, "are the books I have read and/or reread in the last six months or so, and, in one way or another, enjoyed reading. Before deciding upon *The Man Who Knew Coolidge* I considered *Ann Vickers*, *Mantrap*, and *Work of Art*; but *The Man Who Knew Coolidge* won out."

New York Herald Tribune Book Review (22 November 1934), 17. Reprinted with permission of I.H.T. Corporation © New York Herald Tribune.

18 ❧ Dorothy Parker, Hip Pocket Size

I am tempted in writing a piece about this valuable volume to review it as though neither you nor I ever had heard of Dorothy Parker. It might make an interesting stunt. Then on second thought it occurred to me that since Miss Parker's publishers have done such a good production job on this book they might be persuaded to fit me out as an expedition of one to roam the English-speaking world in search of an otherwise literate man or woman to whom the name Dorothy Parker meant nothing whatever. I have no notion where to start this search, and, of course, not the foggiest where it would end.

There is a certain amount of clean, contemptuous fun to be had in trying to dope out where the search would end: the home of John E. Rankin? the Racquet Club? the University of Minnesota? a "phone room" in Jersey City? But these places are ruled out instantly and automatically because one of the rules of the game is to find a literate person who hadn't heard of the lady. And that kills that. However, in fooling around with this idea I have been careful to say "heard of Dorothy Parker"; I didn't say "read Dorothy Parker."

There must be dozens, nay, scores, of busy folk who never have read her. I can think of a switchman on the Erie, for instance, or a research chemist in Michigan, a student nurse in Baltimore, a breaker-boy in Pennsylvania, a Ludlow operator on the *New London Day*, and other workers the nature of whose work keeps them while on the job from reading and, more particularly, turning

Review of *The Portable Dorothy Parker* (New York: Viking, 1944), *The New York Times Book Review* (28 May 1944), 5, 29. —"Dorothy Parker, Hip Pocket Size" © 1944 by The New York Times Company. Reprinted by permission.

the pages of a Parker book and who are so dog-tired (unlike, I may say, my dog) when they get home that all they can do is flop down and go to sleep. It is for these persons, among others, that I would like to write a recommendation of this Dorothy Parker omnibus. In words that they will understand they have a treat in store for them. And those words mean even more to you and me who have read Dorothy Parker, for we know what those others are missing.

I—to choose one of us at random—had read all the stories in this book. I even had read most of the poems. It is my proud boast that to achieve this record was not always so easy as you might think. If word reached me that there was a piece by Dorothy Parker in the *Bookman* I would walk to the public library in my hometown, put my hand over my face so that the girl in charge of fines would not recognize me and track down the rumor. What's more I'd be around a month later on the off chance that there would be more by Dorothy Parker. In due course I had in my possession, either through purchase, gift, or theft, these volumes: *Here Lies, Laments for the Living, After Such Pleasures, Not So Deep as a Well, Enough Rope, Sunset Gun,* and *Death and Taxes.* Now all of these books are available under the one big tent for the small price of $2. And what with the paper shortage I might add "Hur-ree, hur-ree, hur-ree!"

As a bonus or lagniappe Miss Parker has included in her new book five stories and one poem which never before have appeared in book form. The poem is "War Song," which you may have read in Ross's Folly, the weekly magazine which has caught on so well largely through Miss Parker's contributions. The stories are "The Lovely Leave," "The Standard of Living," "Song of the Shirt, 1941," "Mrs. Hofstadter on Josephine Street" and "Cousin Larry."

Of these my favorite is "The Lovely Leave," which is as

topical as a telegram from the War Department and makes me think of an older Parker story, "Here We Are," which, of course, is in the new collection. You go on reading both stories in spite of your awkward, embarrassed sensation of being in a room with two young people, married and in love, who at the moment of all moments ought to be left alone. I guess more than that cannot be said about the goodness of a story.

In reading "The Standard of Living" you become another kind of eavesdropper. It is what J. P. Marquand surely would call the little story of two little stenographers and a little game they play every Saturday afternoon. The little game isn't the newest pastime in the world; it's "What would you do if you had a million dollars?" You played it, I played it and, hell, we *all* played it, but under Miss Parker's direction it becomes brand new—by which I do not mean to compare Miss Parker with Freddy Martin and his romance with Tchaikovsky.

The third of the new five stories is "Song of the Shirt, 1941," which I, somehow, think Miss Parker wrote with one hand. Certainly the artist that she is could have one hand tied behind her and still jab Mrs. Martindale into unconsciousness. Give Miss Parker a silly Lady Bountiful and you will witness a titantic struggle on the general order of Gene Tunney and Tony Galento: interesting as an exhibition of skill, but not much fun.

The fourth of the added starters is "Mrs. Hofstadter on Josephine Street," which is one of the funniest stories in the American language. This in spite of the fact that it is written about a contemptible Negro houseman, which would not seem to be the choicest material for a funny story. Miss Parker, and Miss Parker alone, could have reported (and I'm quite sure it's reporting) on a Horace Wrenn without infuriating Negroes and whites. Horace now belongs with Bonfils and Tabor among my Colorado characters if, as I suspect, the story was written during a brief sojourn Miss Parker made in that aloof State.

As a man who occasionally sweats out a short story, I am glad that the idea for "Cousin Larry," the fifth bonus payment, came to Dorothy Parker and not to me, for I know what I'd have done with it. It is a story that is practically all monologue, one of those in which the talker reveals herself to be the nasty little Bedlington she is. This particular Bedlington naïvely tells how she is lousing up a marriage that couldn't have been anything but ill-starred to begin with. I know no such restraint as Miss Parker exercised and, in exercising it, kept the story from becoming commonplace.

Earlier I spoke of the production job by the publishers. The book will fit, I hope, in many a GI hip pocket, is printed on good stock and typographically is a fine piece of work. There is an index of poem titles and also an index of first lines of poems, of which, by the way, there are about three hundred. There also is an introduction by W. Somerset Maugham, in which he takes many, too many, words to say that he admires Dorothy Parker. In other words, just what I have done.

The book is dedicated to Miss Parker's husband, Lieut. Alan Campbell, USAAF, now overseas.

19 ⚓ That Benny Greenspan

Earlier this year, when I had an office up the hall from Arthur Kober, I used to stop by late in the afternoon to invite my fellow toiler at Ross's Quarry to join me at a nearby workingmen's club, where we could slake the

Review of Arthur Kober's *That Man Is Here Again* (New York: Random House, 1946), *The New York Times Book Review* (8 December 1946), 7, 59. —"That Benny Greenspan" © 1946 by The New York Times Company. Reprinted by permission.

silicosis and curse the bosses. Kober did not always accept these invitations, possibly having learned that it was most often I who did the slaking and cursing, but Kober who ended up with the tab. Other times, though, he would be slapping away at his Underwood and would nod to show he saw me but would shake his head to indicate that he was not to be disturbed. One day I asked him what he was up to, and he told me he was bringing out a book of the Benny Greenspan stories. I thereupon called him a liar and turned on my heel (Benny Greenspan by name). I should have said to him, "I hope you joke," but I didn't think of that till just now.

Perhaps I had better explain why I thought Kober was lying in his white, even teeth. When a *New Yorker* writer brings out a "clip book" he merely asks Miss Thurlow to make up a list of pieces that have not been printed in his earlier books, and she does all the work. In due course the galley proofs arrive from the publisher, the author places them unread in the second drawer of his desk and leaves word at the switchboard that if Random House calls, Mr. Kober (or Gibbs or O'Hara) is out having lunch or cocktails with Harold Guinzburg, president of Viking Press. This is the fear-of-God technique and always works.

Random House stops bothering the author for corrected galleys, and he is allowed to forget all about the book until he sees beautiful full-page advertisements in the *Times* and the *Herald Trib*. The ads are adorned with a photograph taken for the author's prep school yearbook, and a friendly quote from Dorothy Parker which she had intended only for one story in a book published some years back. That, and checking the Canadian sales in the royalty statement, are all the author has to do with bringing out a clip book. Kober therefore obviously was lying when he pretended to be "working" on the Benny Greenspan book. Or so I thought. Actually he was giving the customers better than their money's worth, for he was writing what turns out to be a sprightly comment, usually giving an entertaining anecdote as the source of each and every Greenspan story. I forgive him my debts.

The Benny Greenspan stories are, of course, the *New Yorker* pieces which relate the woeful experiences of Benny Greenspan, Hollywood agent, as told to a party called Artie. Seventeen of the stories have been published in the *New Yorker*, and one was printed someplace else. They are by now what I believe ASCAP calls standards, like, say, "Mother Machree." At the Vine Street Derby, which is the Hollywood Lindy's or at Mike Romanoff's, which is the Beverly Hills Romanoff's, if not the Beverly Hills "21," I am almost certain you could book a table in the name of Benny Greenspan—and Chilios at the Derby, or Joe at Romanoff's, would write it down. The only trouble would be to know whom to seat at the table. Hollywood is so full of Benny Greenspans—life mirroring art—that it would require a table five times as large as the Cabinet's to provide space, and even then there would have to be second sittings.

I know that I have heard many an agent called Benny Greenspan—"that Benny Greenspan," as one would say "that Benedict Arnold" or "that Scrooge." When Budd Schulberg came out with the novel *What Makes Sammy Run?* the field for identification was rather limited and a couple of Hollywood producers even took a kind of inspiration from the character to go on to bigger things. But Sammy was evil, so evil that the master race pirated the novel and used it as an anti-Semitic document. That was as though Winston Churchill had done the same thing with James T. Farrell's Studs Lonigan novels, when W. C. was having his troubles with the Irish.

I forget who said "We have a right to our villains." But Benny is not evil. He is sly, and a chiseler, and an apostle of greed, and financially successful at it, but Kober offers plenty of evidence to show that Greenspan is an unhappy little man. A man's unhappiness does not of itself entitle him to anything, not even pity in many cases, but Kober seems to imply that Benny wishes he could have been something else. And yet I don't believe Kober would like you to think Benny could have been an Einstein.

As an occasional dealer in unpleasant characters of approximately the same racial background as his own, this reviewer has a message for those persons of Jewish ancestry who attack Kober and Schulberg. The message, at full rate, is "Oh, shut up."

20 🖋 The Novels Novelists Read

The Way of All Flesh by Samuel Butler.
Ordeal by Nevil Shute.
Dusty Answer by Rosamund Lehmann.
The Last Tycoon by F. Scott Fitzgerald.
The Old Maid by Edith Wharton.
New Year's Day by Edith Wharton.

For more than two years I have not read any current fiction—novels, that is, and collected short stories— because I have been at work on my own novel. The reason is not only that I have wanted to avoid being influenced, however slightly or subtly, but because I am an extremely slow reader of fiction, and as an author I read new stuff professionally, studiously.

When I come upon a passage I admire, I go back and see how the man (almost always a man) did it. By the same token, I am extremely critical, and I never have been able

"The Novels Novelists Read, or 'Taking in the Washing,'" *The New York Times Book Review* (21 August 1949), 3. © 1949 by The New York Times Company. Reprinted by permission.

to get beyond the first page of one of the most famous novels of our time because the author has made a "weather" mistake (something about snow on the ground) that proves to me he isn't a good writer. There is no relaxation in that kind of reading, and consequently I relax with the newspapers and fact articles in the magazines.

The books I have listed happen to be on my shelves here in the country. It also is an accident of selection that all but one of the books are either English or American-English (Mrs. Wharton), middle and upper-middle-class subject matter. It was not, however, any accident that made me reach for five good writers. Why settle for less?

21 ✎ The Author's Name Is Hemingway

The most important author living today, the outstanding author since the death of Shakespeare, has brought out a new novel. The title of the novel is *Across the River and Into the Trees*. The author, of course is Ernest Hemingway, the most important, the most outstanding author out of the millions of writers who have lived since 1616.

Ernest Hemingway was born in Oak Park, Ill., U.S.A., on July 21, 1898.[1] That makes him an American whose age

Review of Ernest Hemingway's *Across the River and Into the Trees* (New York: Scribner's, 1950), *The New York Times Book Review* (10 September 1950), 1, 30–31. —"The Author's Name is Hemingway" © 1950 by The New York Times Company. Reprinted by permission. This review generated considerable controversy, and O'Hara was misquoted as having claimed that *Across the River and Into the Trees* was the greatest work since Shakespeare.

1. Hemingway was born in 1899.

is fifty-two. His father was a physician named Clarence Edmonds Hemingway; his mother's maiden name was Grace Hall.

Hemingway went to Oak Park High and not to college. He got into the newspaper business, went to France as a Red Cross ambulance driver when he was nineteen years old and a year later was badly shot up in Italy. After World War I he spent most of his time in Europe, with visits to the United States and Africa for hunting, fishing, and seeing friends and acquaintances.

He anticipated World War II, and took part in the actions in Spain. In 1944 he participated in the invasion of the European continent. (He was anti-Fascist in the Spanish hostilities and anti-Hitler in the subsequent activities. It may seem that these things should go without saying, but nowadays nothing goes without saying. These comments are meant to be straightforward, but there must be no lingering doubt.)

Between War One and War Two Ernest Hemingway produced the following books: *Three Stories and Ten Poems* (1923); *In Our Time* (1924); *The Torrents of Spring* (1926); *The Sun Also Rises* (1926); *Men Without Women* (1927); *A Farewell to Arms* (1929); *Death in the Afternoon* (1932); *Winner Take Nothing* (1933); *The Green Hills of Africa* (1935); *To Have and Have Not* (1937); *The Fifth Column* (1938); *For Whom the Bell Tolls* (1940).

Books do not necessarily represent an author's activity, but the new novel is Hemingway's thirteenth book in what appears to be twenty-seven years of writing and knocking around, for a rough average of one book every two years. Hemingway has not been idle, and most of the items in his bibliography come alive by merely calling up their titles.

The reasons that Ernest Hemingway is important are not easy to search for, although they are easy to find. Once you have skipped the remarks of the pedants, the college professors, the litterateurs, and of Hemingway himself, and have examined his background and his still immediate history, you can relax down to the fine, simple, inexplicable acceptance of being in the world-presence of a genius. The college professors (no can do; can teach pretty good) are ready out of their chunky erudition to prove that Ernest Hemingway got that way because he had a sister whose middle name was Xerxes. Or they, the pundits, may have got by hearsay a remote rumor that one day in Montreal a man who looked very much like Ernest Hemingway was seen to have in the left-hand pocket of his tweed jacket a small volume not too dissimilar from an *Anabasis*.

The chances are that Ernest Hemingway in the formative years didn't read much but Ring Lardner's sport stories in the Chicago papers, Caesar's Gallic Wars and the literature that any high school boy skips over. Over or through. He was a big kid with not very good eyesight, with enormous, ill-controlled strength of muscle, and, apparently, an enviable admiration for an enviable father. Ernest went to the rehearsal war, and, after it, got some rude experience in cablese, a frustrating discipline that almost lost us all an artist. There was, it must be remembered, a phase during which Hemingway could have been found guilty of poetry of a sort.

Miss Gertrude Stein, who was as inevitable as the Albany night boat, did Hemingway no harm. She was living in Paris, France, and she was a good influence. I have a theory, which I have offered before, that all you need to know about the influence of Miss Stein on the young Ernest Hemingway is to pretend that you are, say, a Chinese who never has read English: you look at some pages of the *Autobiography of Alice B. Toklas*, then look at the superb Caporetto retreat writing in *A Farewell to Arms*. You will think they were written by the same person.

In the new novel (as in some earlier ones) the big block paragraph is not employed by the artist as it was in *A Farewell to Arms*. I have not been able to find a paragraph longer than fourteen uninterrupted slugs of type. Whatever influence Gertrude Stein had on Hemingway has been accepted, studied, utilized, and rejected. Ernest Hemingway is and really always was, his own man. We now can forget about Gertrude Stein. Thank you very much, and so long.

The outsize boy, the doctor's son, the brittle bones, the halting speech (completely different from that of Dr. Maugham), the defective eyesight—they all had and have their part in the mental and physical makeup of a great author. But who has not known a stammering, gangling gawk of a doctor's embarrassment who couldn't go past M in the alphabet? Ernest Hemingway, the sternly self-edited artist, had young people in the 1930s marrying on no more than "We'll have a fine life." Why? Because Ernest Hemingway, the artist, had put just those words in his lines of type at just the right time.

The truculent, self-pitying hero of *Across the River and Into the Trees* is a busted one-star general called Col. Richard Cantwell. He seems to have traversed the same territory as the charming Lieutenant Henry of *A Farewell to Arms*. It is impossible to believe that the lieutenant and the colonel are the same man, and therefore the autobiographical aspect must be ruled out one time or the other. The present reviewer, whose age is forty-five, is unwilling to concede that Enrico and Ricardo are the same infant with years piled on. In any event, Colonel Cantwell is in Venice to see his girl, a beautiful and quite incredible countess named Renata. The colonel is full of junk, against the bad heart condition he has, and the story is hardly more than a report of their last love-making, to the accompaniment of a threnody on and by the dying warrior. That great, great man and fine actor, Walter Huston, was in my mind all the time I read this book. Huston, singing "September Song," you know. But Hemingway, the inimitable, has written a 308-page novel out of a "September Song" situation, and not one syllable of what Hemingway has written can or will be missed by any literate person in the world.

Before you ever see the girl, the countess, you are taken through some duck-shooting that makes you want to let go at a boatman with both barrels. At the same time you somehow are rooting for a second duck. The colonel is understandably angry with the inefficient boatman; he also is rather swaggeringly proud of getting two ducks. I, myself, a rifle man, wanted to kill the colonel while he was in the barrel that you shot ducks from, but that certainly is nothing against Hemingway's writing. He probably meant it that way.

The novel opens with the colonel on his way to his ultimate rendezvous with the countess. Cantwell, the colonel, is pulling rank on the rather nice little T–5 who is driving the colonel's Cadillac.[2] The little fellow is somebody named Jackson, from the state of Wyoming. My own personal experience with Wyoming characters has been that Jackson would have twirled the colonel out of the automobile and reported him dead. The colonel insists upon giving Jackson, a noncommissioned officer, a Michelin-Baedeker course in how to appreciate Venice, Italy. The course goes back quite a few years, several centuries, in fact. It not only had to do with the colonel's serving in the Italian Army in War One, but 'way, 'way before. Jackson, who seemed to the present reviewer to be one of those Wyoming skinny boys whose father might have been a pal of Senator Cary's, should have stopped

2. Colonel Cantwell has a Buick.

the Cadillac and said, "Colonel, you got any prayers, you say them, because you bore me." Then, to be sure, we'd have had no novel. Or not the same novel.

After the patronizing travelog, the noncom and Colonel Cantwell get to Venice, and the colonel has the rendez-vous with his girl, the countess. She is, on this reviewer's oath, practically all that a middle-aged man with a cardiac condition could ask for. Not yet nineteen years old, a countess who need not worry about consequences, Re-nata (whose name sounds like lasso to me) is so much in love with the colonel that she takes his rudeness and gives him emeralds in return.

It is so easy to kid that aspect of Hemingway's writing and it is so foolish to do so. Go ahead and disbelieve in Catherine Barkley, as I disbelieve now in the Countess Renata, as I did too in Maria, of *For Whom the Bell Tolls*. But the Hemingway heroines, as distinguished from the Sinclair Lewis ones, have a way of catching up with you after you have passed them by. You read them; you see them played by Helen Hayes, Elissa Landi, Ingrid Bergman; you put them away. And yet in later years you form your own nontheatrical picture of them out of what you remember of what Hemingway wrote, and what you have seen of living women. If Rita Hayworth or Ava Gardner should play Renata it will be easy to understand why either actress was cast, but it will probably only postpone a personal picture of the heroine of *Across the River and Into the Trees*. There are not many real things about Renata, in fact, she has so few individual charac-teristics and attributes that after the inevitable movie has been made, it may be much easier to form your own idea—and almost entirely your own—of what Renata was intended to be.

It is not unfair or unjustifiable, this casting of the novel's characters. The novel was written as a serial for *Cosmopolitan*, whose demands and restrictions are, I should say, almost precisely those of the movies. Now that the novel is available between boards, a great many touches that most likely were in Hemingway's working manuscript have been restored. They don't add much, they don't take much away. At the same time they do make a difference, they make the bound volume authentically Hemingway, and not Hemingway plus (or maybe minus is the word) the *Cosmopolitan* editors. And in any case the touches never would appear in the movies. They would not even appear in the most rudimentary "treatment" that might be submitted to the Johnston Office.

The reasons Hemingway is important are not easy to search for, but they are easy to find. They are hard to search for, because he is so competent and deceivingly simple and plain. It is not enough to say that simplicity itself is rare. People are always mailing authors their nine-year-old children's compositions as examples of beautiful simplicity. Simplicity is not rare. And fancy, complicated writing isn't rare either. Every author gets fancy writing in the form of letters and manuscripts from jailbirds, psychopaths, and students.

But what Hemingway has—and Steinbeck has it too—is pre-paper discipline. It means, first of all, point of view. A great many nonwriters have it without having to reveal it, but with an author it is not only revealing; it often is exposing. A possibly oversimplified definition of point of view would be "feeling and preference" and, in an author's case, the expression of an attitude. It is in the manner and method of the expression of the attitude that writers vary, and before that, the pre-paper discipline— the thinking, the self-editing—gets its test.

An author may seem to lead a ruggedly simple life, but the fact that he is an author makes him not a simple individual. The personality therefore requires enormous discipline in putting the uncomplicated thinking down on paper. The ostensibly simple lives led by men like

Hemingway and Steinbeck tell practically nothing about the personalities, although the writing is simple too. The ostensibly simple life led by William Faulkner tells nothing about him either, for the writing comes out plain but complicated, with so little change in the process between first thought and final printed page that Faulkner, while a genius, may not be an artist. It makes damn small difference to him or to me.

It shouldn't to Hemingway, although it may, because he permits himself practically no private life, or at any rate gets none. The most recent, and most disgusting, example of the intrustions into Hemingway's private life was made by a publication that reported on Hemingway's drinking habits, somewhat in the manner of a gleeful parole officer. It also included some direct quotes, in tin-ear fashion, of what were passed off as Hemingway's speech, but sounded more like the dialogue written for the Indian chief in *Annie Get Your Gun*.

The inability to write the way people talk is a common affliction among writers. But for Eustace Tilley to raise an eyeglass over anybody's drinking is one for the go-climb-a-lamppost department. The magazine had printed numerous little attacks on Hemingway by a semi-anonymous staffman who has gone to his heavenly reward, just as it printed attacks on Faulkner by a critic who has returned to his proper chore on the radio. With the long piece on Hemingway the magazine achieved a new low in something.

In the new novel, Hemingway, rather regrettably, has done nothing to protect himself against personal attack, or, more accurately, counterattack. He has named some names, and made easily identifiable some others: Patton, Eisenhower, Montgomery, Ney, Custer, Truman, Dewey, as well as an author or two, a journalist or two, and probably a few noncelebrated individuals who will recognize themselves or think they do.

This does not sound like a *roman à clef*, any more than it is an autobiography (Hemingway is still alive, and Dick Cantwell ends the book by dying), and that doesn't matter either way. What matters is that Ernest Hemingway has brought out a new book.

To use his own favorite metaphor, he may not be able to go the full distance, but he can still hurt you. Always dangerous. Always in there with that right cocked.

Real class.

22 ✒ My Ten Favorite Plays

The novelist, short-story writer and playwright, whose connection with the legitimate theatre also includes service as a critic, has made the following selections:

1. *Pal Joey*
2. *Holiday*
3. *Chee-Chee*
4. *The Petrified Forest*
5. *Journey's End*
6. *Street Scene*
7. *Serena Blandish*
8. *Our Town*
9. *Of Thee I Sing*
10. *X*

Amplifying the cryptic tenth selection, Mr. O'Hara adds: "The X, of course, is for a play by a playwright friend I've overlooked."

"My Ten Favorite Plays," *Theatre Arts*, 41 (November 1957), 9.

Interviews and Public Statements

23 🖹 John O'Hara, Who Talks Like His Stories

Robert Van Gelder

John O'Hara said that when quite young he had made up his mind that he would write three novels—one about his hometown of Pottsville, Pa., one about New York, and one about Hollywood. In 1933, twenty-eight years old, he decided that it was time to get started, so he went on the wagon and commenced to write. But the Pottsville material at first took the form of a series of long, integrated short stories and he hadn't gone very far before he decided that he was trying to cheat himself.

"That was in August. I was in Pittsburgh working on what was laughingly called a news magazine. I got out of there and came back to New York—tried to make a living free-lancing mainly to the *New Yorker* and *Harper's Bazaar*. I threw over the short-story idea in December and began on a novel, living in a $9-a-week room in a place called the Pickwick Arms. There was no desk—only a chair, a bureau, and the bed. I used the bed as a desk—put my typewriter on it—and each night I'd work until my back began to hurt.

"My working time is late at night. Evenings I'd go to Tony's and sit around drinking coffee and talking to people until about midnight, then go back to my room and write. Sometimes I'd quit after a paragraph or two, but usually I keep going until about 7 o'clock.

"John O'Hara Who Talks Like His Stories" by Robert Van Gelder, *The New York Times Book Review* (26 May 1940), 12. © 1940 by The New York Times Company. Reprinted by permission.

"The novel interested me and after a while I discovered that I had only $3 and that because I'd spent all my time on the novel I had no short pieces out—that is, there was no chance of a sale that would bring in some cash. This worried me. I was not so good on the touch, either, because I owed a lot of people.

"I had 25,000 words of the novel completed. At various times in the last few years three publishers had seen my short pieces and asked me—well, said that if I wrote a novel they'd like to see it. I wrote three identical letters saying that I had 25,000 words written and that I'd submit the manuscript under two conditions. The first condition was that if they liked it they would subsidize me while I finished it. The second condition was that they'd read the manuscript overnight.

"I finished these letters early in the morning, put them in the mail and came up to Times Square and went to the movies. I spent the whole day in 10 and 15 cent movie houses along Forty-second Street. When I went back to my room about 5:30 that afternoon I found messages to call all three publishers. There was nothing wrong with the mails that day—Cap Pearce of Harcourt, Brace had read my letter and called me at 11:30 that morning. His had been the first call, so I telephoned him and he said that he'd read the 25,000 words that night. The next day he telephoned to say that Harcourt, Brace wanted the book and to ask how big a subsidy I needed. I told him I wanted $50 a week for three months and he said to come over and sign the papers."

O'Hara completed *Appointment in Samarra* within four days of his self-imposed deadline. The book was unquestionably first rate and well before publication a movie contract was offered and accepted and O'Hara went to Hollywood as a writer for Paramount. Much of his time since then he has been under Hollywood contract. His

Hollywood rating is that of a "polish guy." That is, in general he works on scripts that already are partly completed but require dialogue or comedy angles.

His Hollywood novel *Hope for Heaven* was an effort to show the young people of its year just as they were, to compass in a brief book the current moral attitude, the manner of speech, the political view, the type of humor that appealed—in short, youth in an America temporarily stunted. The book brought him a number of letters from people of college age asking him how old he was—a sound indication that the novel had accomplished its purpose.

O'Hara's next novel will have as its central figure an older woman. He is in New York now working on the book of a musical show based upon his "Pal Joey" stories —they have been appearing in the *New Yorker.*When he finishes this he intends to write a play—a tragedy. And next year he will start work on his fourth novel, a story of encroaching age. Meanwhile he has completed a number of sketches and short stories that will appear in magazines this summer.

Tall, with good shoulders and capable hands, O'Hara is not a man to avoid arguments. His energy is sufficient to form a basis for legend—old friends recall the night some years ago when, feeling that a soldier had insulted him, he made a determined attempt to reach Governors Island with the intention of taking on the army.

His talk is spiced with an entirely agreeable note of challenge that, as it has no itch of nervousness about it, merely adds to the interest. Blessed with a really magnificent memory and an unerring instinct for vivid and significant detail, his talk has much of the quality of his writing. The fact that his writing is all first draft, that it goes to the printer just as it comes from his typewriter, becomes readily believable after an hour or so of talk.

24 ✎ The Only Good Thing I Ever Got Out of Booze

Earl Wilson

Edgar Allan Poe, the Lush of Literature, wrote while all canned up, but up till press time today, nobody's been able to do it since. John O'Hara and I talked of this at a bar. O'Hara, a pretty good boy with the juice, practically came out for prohibition for writers while they're working.

He looked along the bar and noted it was full, as were some of the people at it, except at the far end, where there was a hole.

"Up here, huh?" He pointed with a jerk of his head. We put our elbows on the bar, and he said to the barman, "Orange blossom."

With what-the-hell in his voice, he added, "Double."

I liked the look of the guy, who's bigger-shouldered than I'd expected, healthy-looking, with a big square Irish kisser and face that's clean and plain, like he writes.

"If I write any extended work," he finally said, "I gotta god damn well get offa the booze."

I quietly slid my notebook on the bar. As an ex-reporter, he couldn't help asking, "Do you think the notebook makes them clam up? I would say half of them do clam up."

"You can't say you didn't tell me if I write it down."

"Right," he said. "Then I have no beef. Well, I'm going to level with you about *Pal Joey*. You are a guy that's got to be on the eerie, and you heard I wrote it while I was on the sauce. I didn't. I was sober."

O'Hara, surely one of our greatest writers, sipped from

New York Post (28 March 1946), 41. Published in Earl Wilson's syndicated column, "It Happened Last Night." Reprinted by permission. The title has been supplied by the editor.

the glass, appreciatively, and then said, "This is strictly cufferoo advice to writers. This story.

"My wife and I were back from England. Broke.

"We were living at my mother-in-law's. At 93d and 5th. I tell you 93d and 5th because that's important. Do you feel like another one? I think I had better eat something."

He ordered a sandwich. "I had an idea for a story. I said to my wife I'd go to Philadelphia. Hole up in the Hotel Ben Franklin a couple days, lock myself in, eat on room service. Just work.

"But the night before, we went out, and I got stiff.

"I got up next morning to start to the station, and I am dying.

"Now as we got to the Pierre, at 60th St., I said to the cab, 'Stop here.' I went in. After a drink or two, I feel what-the-hell. Better take a nap. I check in.

"Then," said O'Hara, looking down at the table, shaking his head, "began a real beauty. Just getting stiff and passing out. I started Thursday. By Saturday morning I'd drunk myself sober. I picked up the phone and said, 'What time is it?'

"The girl says, 'Quarter after 7.'

"I asked her, 'A.M. or P.M.?' The girl said, 'A.M. and the day is Saturday.' They knew me there.

"At that point remorse set in. I asked, 'What kind of god damn heel am I? I must be worse'n anybody in the world.' Then I figured, 'No, there must be somebody worse than me—but who?' Al Capone, maybe. Then I got it—maybe some nightclub masters of ceremonies I know."

O'Hara took a cigaret from his handsome gold case. "That was my idea. I went to work and wrote a piece about a nightclub heel in the form of a letter. I finished the piece by 11 o'clock. I went right home.

"Now I'd never been south of 60th St.

"I said to my wife, 'I have a confession to make.'"

His wife said, "No, you haven't; you've been to the Pierre."

"How did she know? Instinctively, I guess. The *New Yorker* bought the story the same day, ordered a dozen more, and then came the play, and the movie. . . . [1]

"That was the only good thing I ever got out of booze, but mind you, Wilson, I wasn't on a bender at the time I wrote it. I was perfectly sober! Have you got that down in your notebook?

"Orange blossom," he said to the barman. "Double."

25 🔖 Talk With John O'Hara
Harvey Breit

As has been said before, John O'Hara (whose new book *A Rage to Live* has been stirring up the literary and psychiatric factions) was a jack of all trades and a master of some—being at various times a steel-mill roughneck, a soda-jerk, secretary to Heywood Broun, and guard in an amusement park. As well as a pretty fair newspaperman. Now Mr. O'Hara isn't scattering himself about; he's strictly a writer and, as all hands agree (even if they disagree about the new book), a pretty fair one, too.

Mr. O'Hara looks less the writer than the steel-mill roughneck he once was. That, of course, is in the tradition of American writers who, it seems, just don't like to *look* like writers. He's a big guy with powerful wrists and hands and carries an overall noncorpulent weight of 205 pounds. He looks as if he could do all right in a brawl

1. The movie of *Pal Joey* was not made until 1957.

"Talk with John O'Hara" by Harvey Breit, *The New York Times Book Review* (4 September 1949), 11. © 1949 by The New York Times Company. Reprinted by permission.

either with man or bear. He is also doing all right just as a literary fellow—the Book Find Club has taken *A Rage to Live* as its September choice.

Mr. O'Hara was naturally interested in talking about his controversial new book. "I couldn't have written it," he said, "at the time I did *Appointment in Samarra*. I wrote *Samarra* in '33. But all the while I wanted a hell of a lot to write the other novel, the novel that any guy wants to write who has lived in a town just short of being New York, Los Angeles, Philadelphia, or Boston.

"In these towns there is always a family, not necessarily the richest one but the snappiest one, that sets the tone in manners, sure, but also in cars and horses. Say, thirty-five years ago, there would be one snappy family, and they would put their money into a hunter rather than into a Marmon or a Pierce."

Did Mr. O'Hara consider *A Rage to Live* a departure from his earlier work? "Yes," Mr. O'Hara said. "The earlier books were special books about specialized people; but this is the big one, the overall one."

Mr. O'Hara, having been a newspaperman, undoubtedly was aware of the argument about whether the occupational hazards of the fourth estate had beneficial or disastrous effects on the creative novelist. What, one wanted to know, were Mr. O'Hara's findings? "The newspaper influence," Mr. O'Hara said, "is a good one for the writer. It teaches economy of words. It makes you write faster. When you're on rewrite as I was, you can't fool around at half-past nine trying to write beautiful lacy prose."

Mr. O'Hara wasn't the one, obviously, for a rich or luscious (or lacy) metaphor. "Prose writing in 1949 I don't think should be anything but accurate. I keep away from figures of speech. I can compare my car [a low-slung, fireman's red British toy of a car] with my favorite horse—War Admiral. I love them both and they're little and fast. But the comparison wouldn't go very far because there's no clash of temperament between a four-cylinder English car that I drive as there is between me and a horse I might ride, especially at my current weight."

Mr. O'Hara then quit his vehicular illustration. "It's the workman that I like in literature," he said. "I like John Steinbeck because he works all the time. . . . Who else do I admire? Like everybody else, I'm looking forward to that Hemingway book like a kid waiting for the fourth of July. I don't think the Pulitzer Prize was ever more deserved than by James Gould Cozzens—and he's one man I don't know. Of course, I admire work when it isn't work per se—when it's good work is what I mean. Faulkner is the genius—the only genius so far as I'm concerned."

Would Mr. O'Hara try to tell why? "This is not the standard thing," he replied. "The reason Faulkner's work is so good is that so much of it stays. I happen to know Faulkner writes practically on the head of a pin; his calligraphy is so small he could write one of his long chapters on a single piece of copy paper."

One wondered whether this interesting biographical fact was relevant. Mr. O'Hara said, smilingly, that perhaps it wasn't. However, it did finally turn out to have a connection with what he meant by Faulkner's genius. "Knowing Faulkner as well and as slightly as I do, it seems to me there is no awkward transition from the brain to the printed page. Whereas some of us lose from the thinking to the ultimate work."

"Did you know," Mr. O'Hara asked, "that one of the reasons you don't get flora in my work is that I'm color-blind? I probably can't identify six flowers. But I can identify everything on a farm (my father had one). I can tell you all the differences between a Guernsey and a Jersey (anybody can tell a Holstein). I can tell by the texture of the milk."

There are more darned things in Mr. O'Hara, this interviewer concluded, than were dreamed of in his philosophy.

26 ✍ How Do I Write?

John O'Hara

How do I write? I write on the typewriter, not pen or pencil, but from notes which I keep in notebooks and put down in engineering-style printing with a fountain pen.

How do I play? Well, if you mean play-not-work, I play golf. I gave up tennis six years ago when I reached forty. We live in Princeton and go to the Philadelphia Orchestra every other Friday to listen to the world's finest band. I used to play bridge, but now I play backgammon. I used to be a fairly good bridge player; I am a lousy backgammon player, as certain members of the Nassau Club will attest. When we go to New York—less and less frequently—I check in at "21" and leave there only when the night watchman comes on.

As to reading: I read the fact articles in the magazines: I take the *Trib*, the *Times*, the *Journal-American*, the *Post*, and the *Philadelphia Inquirer*. I also read the *Wall Street Journal* and the *Trenton Times* at the Nassau Club. I read practically no new fiction unless I have been asked to review same. I am never without the works of Sir Arthur Conan Doyle. I am interested in American history and geography. I stick my neck out by saying I probably know this country, the whole of it, as well as any man alive. Almost my favorite reading is *Who's Who*, then *The World*

New York Herald Tribune Book Review (7 October 1951), 6. Reprinted with permission of the I.H.T. Corporation © New York Herald Tribune. The title has been supplied by the editor.

Almanac, then *The Social Register*, but there is a big gap between *Who's Who* and *The World Almanac*. I have every *Who's Who* since 1934, and I observe the changes the subjects make from one volume to another.

As to my ways, they are peculiar (Kipling?). I seem to have settled down a bit, but that is not to say that I do not have an occasional outburst. I am married and have a six-year-old daughter with the mellifluous name, Wylie O'Hara. I am a very lucky man, but by God I earned it.

I am against two things: cruelty and stupidity—and they are not the same. For an extension of this remark see my new book.

The only other thing I wanted to be is ship's surgeon (my father was a surgeon).

So much for the well-known pronoun.

27 ✍ Talk With John O'Hara

Lewis Nichols

Pottsville, industrial city (pop. 24,530) co. seat of Schuylkill co., E. Pa. . . . NW of Reading . . . settled c. 1780, laid out 1816 . . . grew with the advent of extensive anthracite mining . . . a rallying place for the Molly Maguires. . . .

Thus the Columbia Encyclopedia, in the brisk manner of lexicographers counting the trees while overlooking a fine south forty stand of forest. For Pottsville, along with everything else including the Molly Maguires, is Gibbsville. No one makes any bones about this, least of all

"Talk with John O'Hara" by Lewis Nichols, *The New York Times Book Review* (27 November 1955), 16. © 1955 by The New York Times Company. Reprinted with permission.

John O'Hara, ex-citizen of one and manipulating boss of the other.

In conversation Mr. O'Hara has a tendency to use the names interchangeably. Speaking of some incident of boyhood, he can mention Gibbsville, then correct to Pottsville. Speaking of *Ten North Frederick*, the name of his new novel as well as a thoroughfare in Gibbsville, he can inadvertently call it by its Pottsville name. Since Fort Penn, a 50-mile distant neighbor, is also Harrisburg, the whole SE section of the Commonwealth of Pennsylvania becomes a patchwork of what is and what isn't. Only Mr. O'Hara, with pen quicker than the eye, can keep them apart, serenely.

"Gibbsville is my Yoknapatawpha County," he remarked. "The physical design is that of Pottsville, as it exists. I left there in '27, when I was twenty-two; before that had been away at school for four years. But there were a solid eighteen years of impressions, which I've gone back and referred to. But what it amounts to is that I've just taken a real town and made it conform to a novelist's idea.

"I used to think Lewis's Zenith was Buffalo. I'd have had a hard time being convinced it wasn't Buffalo. It wasn't, of course, but was his own invention. A novelist is lucky to create a place like Zenith or Gibbsville. He can fill it with people of his own invention, and can go on inventing. I could do a novel a year for twenty-five years on Gibbsville."

Mr. O'Hara's current home is in Princeton, N.J., a central point from which he can commute to Broadway, Hollywood, or way stations. A tall man, he slouches over several chairs. In addition to books, his study shows a nice taste in saluting cannons, trophies, and, inexplicably, outsize flashlights. There is a Gibbsville corner, with old pictures and maps of Pottsville, and he plans presently to unfurl a Pennyslvania state flag there.

Since Gibbsville is Pottsville, and Pottsville is peopled, do Pottsville people ever take exception to Mr. O'Hara's muse?

"They try to pinpoint the figures, but not successfully, because the characters have two patterns. One is superficial—clothes, schools, social positions, jobs. The other is psychological. Julian English, of *Appointment in Samarra* was, superficially, two or three fellows. On the psychological side, he happened to be a guy I knew living on the wrong side of the tracks.

"Everyone in Harrisburg recognized Grace of *A Rage To Live*. But on the psychological side she actually was someone living in another state, and not even superficially was she Pennsylvania. In *Ten North Frederick*, Joe Chapin isn't comparable to anyone in Gibbsville—Pottsville—but there are a few points of resemblance to several people.

"You're on pretty sound ground if you start out with a life you know about. Then, given no extremes—abject poverty, say—the psychological pattern is suitable for dressing in the superficial clothes of a cut or two above. I do a lot of family tree stuff. In this book there are a good many people I never dealt with before. I put down in great detail such things as births, dates, marriages, and children. Some may be mentioned only once, but I'm a damn sight better off if I know all about them."

Although he could write a Gibbsville novel a year for twenty-five years, Mr. O'Hara will not. "With a middle-class conscience which makes me worry when I take a week off," he now is primarily engrossed in a play and in the book for a musical show. There also is movie work as well as a column in *Collier's*.

"You get a great satisfaction from a book," he said. "You know your reader is captive inside those covers, but as a novelist you have to imagine the satisfaction he's getting. Now in the theatre—well, I used to drop in during both productions of *Pal Joey* and watch, not imagine, the people enjoy it.

"I'd willingly start my next novel—about a small town—right now, but I know I need the diversion of a play. This will let me store up excitement—in order to drain myself of whatever I have to have to write a book."

Continuing on the O'Hara agenda is a narrative poem about a jazz drummer and to be told in several jazz beats.

"I've fooled around with that for ten years," he said a little mournfully. "But I know when it's ready I'll write it."

28 ✒ John O'Hara From Pottsville, Pa.

John K. Hutchens

The first reviews of his new novel, *Ten North Frederick*, were in, and by a comfortable margin they were appreciative, and John O'Hara clearly was pleased. It hasn't always been so. A Pennsylvania Irishman who believes in answering his critics, he has been known to file lacerating dissents when the opportunity arose, but now he was easy and relaxed in the trophy-filled, book-lined study of his home on the edge of the Princeton campus. One of the reviews said flatly that this was his best book, better even than the one he began with (*Appointment in Samarra*), and Mr. O'Hara agreed. It isn't exactly news when an author says his latest book is his best, but even his critics have never accused Mr. O'Hara of not meaning what he said, whether they liked it or not.

He was the happier about it, a visitor guessed, because *Ten North Frederick* had gone precisely according to

New York Herald Tribune Book Review (4 December 1955), 2. Reprinted with permission of I.H.T. Corporation © New York Herald Tribune.

schedule, an old O'Hara custom. Months ago he set a deadline, August 1, when the last of his manuscript would be delivered. It was delivered on August 1, by which time the earlier portions of the book were being put into type. No margin of time for editing? the visitor asked.

"None," said Mr. O'Hara. "I won't sit still for any editing by any publishing house. It would be different with a biography. I'd welcome factual corrections there. But in fiction, in a novel, if there are mistakes, they're going to be *my* mistakes." Style, he said, didn't enter into it. "I don't feel myself a stylist, but I have a presentation, as Joe Hergesheimer did—to choose a very opposite example."

One factor in that schedule, of course, is that he is a fast-writing, one-draft writer, now as he was when he was a newspaperman. "I pride myself," he said, "on never having missed a deadline. I have failed to show up for work, and separated myself from a job that way. But if a story was due at 10:10, I had it all in by 10:09." Another, even more important factor: "If I may say so, I have an instinct for knowing how much I can do in a certain amount of time, and how much I want to say."

Still, in the case of *Ten North Frederick*, it must have taken some special doing. He started on the writing a year ago this month, worked fast for three months (he took the manuscript with him on his wedding trip in January), went to Hollywood for awhile to talk about doing a screen original ("because I needed money"), came back to Princeton and wrote his screen original by day, his novel by night, with three days out every other week for his *Collier's* column, "Appointment With O'Hara." He would not, he admits, care to do it again.

In his new novel, as in his first one, he is back in Gibbsville, Pa., which is to say Pottsville, Pa., his native town. Street by street, his visitor asked, are the two towns the same? They are, said Mr. O'Hara. "The across-the-tracks stuff, the canal, the railroad, are where I have placed them. Ethnologically, too, as well as topographically, I have stayed close to the facts of Pottsville." This doesn't mean, he went on to say, that he has drawn Pottsville citizens to the life (though some of them think so—others resent his not including them). A very few minor characters are all but photographed—"to populate a party, say. But beyond that, or above it, I go in for disguises. I use the psychological pattern of a real person, then cover him up with the superficial aspects of another."

The talk went back across the years—to the old *Morning Telegraph*, where, under the name of "Franey Delaney," he was one of the first radio columnists, though he had no radio and was obliged to do his homework in a radio-equipped saloon; to Hollywood, where he first went in 1934 and had his option renewed because he could talk horses and football to his producer; to his early story-writing days for the *New Yorker*, with which he broke in 1949 over that magazine's review of *A Rage to Live* (but he speaks with real gratitude of its great editor, Harold Ross, who taught him something about the importance of clarity in writing); to the nightclubs where his hoofer-heel, Pal Joey, originated, and the vastly successful musical that bears that hoofer's name.

And there was the memorable day when, down to his last few dollars in a hall bedroom, and with 25,000 words of *Appointment in Samarra* written, he sent identical special delivery letters to three publishers, promising the book to the first one that answered. He sat through the day at a movie house, came back to find that all three firms had phoned, and sent his manuscript to Harcourt, Brace. "Young man, do you know where you are going?" asked

Alfred Harcourt, meaning did Mr. O'Hara know how the novel was coming out. Mr. O'Hara did, and got $500 down and $50 a week until the book was done.

Seven years resident in Princeton, he says that the nightclubs are out of his life now. "But they are out of everybody's life—I mean, the young actors and writers who used to be the nightclub cadre. The kids don't sit up all night any more. They're more interested in security." Sensible, perhaps, but inhibiting. Mr. O'Hara, of whom someone said that he spent more time in nightclubs than in bed, now comes into New York only once in two weeks, to see a show or two and in general to hold the franchise as an alumnus.

For the rest, in his quiet, hard-working life in Princeton he reads six New York daily papers, seven magazines, very little modern fiction; spends a good deal of time poring over *Who's Who* and the *World Almanac*, follows Princeton athletics, returns frequently to F. Scott Fitzgerald and Arthur Conan Doyle, awaits the production of a play he has written called "The Sisters," drives a six-year-old, right-hand-drive MG, and seems mellower than he once was toward people he used not to like.

"If you're fifty and philosophical——" said Mr. O'Hara. "I'm one, and trying to be other."

29 ✒ As *From the Terrace* Goes to Press: Appointment With O'Hara

John O'Hara was in fine spirits when we called on him one warm October afternoon at his Princeton home.

Reprinted by permission of R. R. Bowker Company, publisher of *Publishers Weekly* 174 (3 November 1958), 22–23. Copyright © by R. R. Bowker Company.

His new novel, *From the Terrace*, by far his most ambitious (900 pages) and significant work to date, was going through the mechanical steps preliminary to publication on November 27 by Random House. Mr. O'Hara, as the trade knows, acts as his own literary agent ("In my days on newspapers, I learned to read a contract as well as an agent can," he told us, "and why should I turn over the 10 percent?"), and in this capacity he had just concluded a movie deal with Twentieth Century-Fox for *From the Terrace* on a cash-plus-percentage basis said to be the highest ever granted by the studio (*PW*, October 20).

From the Terrace, Mr. O'Hara said, was finished a year ahead of his schedule for it and will be published three years to the day after the publication of *Ten North Frederick*, the author's last major work. The actual typewriting of the book took two years of eight-hours-a-day effort ("When I'm ready to write a book, I sit down and write it straight through"), and the preliminary research took a lot longer. The book has more than one hundred characters, ranges all around the United States in setting, and covers the first half of this century, a period which Mr. O'Hara regards as the most exciting in the world's history. "There was a lot of detail research for this book," he said, "World War I Navy stuff, for instance, and getting chronology right." Plus, of course, the O'Hara hallmark of detailed description of the appurtenances of life in any given period. As a social historian, he always is aware, for example, of what sort of person would drive a Packard, what sort would buy a Pierce-Arrow.

Why does he regard *From the Terrace* as his best book? In addition to the richness of the time it is concerned with and the quality of detail that is in it, Mr. O'Hara cited the construction of the plot and, specifically, the techniques employed to deal with chronology (including flashbacks within flashbacks among its other devices). "The experience I've had with writing two fairly big books, *Rage to*

Live and *Ten North Frederick*, enabled me to write this one. *Rage to Live* was going to be my first book, but it took me fifteen years as a writer to gain the experience to write a big book. Now I'm fifty-three years old, and I think I've gained the wisdom needed to handle a really big novel about a big subject. In the past, critics of my work have started with *Appointment in Samarra* and worked forward. Now, I think they'll start with *From the Terrace* and look back."

With Mr. O'Hara, research can start in the form of almost idle curiosity. A citation in a book of an obscure but important and profitable industrial process leads to explorations of what the process is and who invented it and profited from it. A three-line cryptic mention in *Who's Who* leads to inquiries on Wall Street. "If the man is on a board of directors," Mr. O'Hara said, "the chances are that I'll know someone else on that board. There are few people who know this country better than I do. I know every important person in this country, or I know someone close to each of them." A great amount of the research Mr. O'Hara does in his own library, a fine small reference collection to which the *Dictionary of American Biography* has recently been added. ("I splurged," is Mr. O'Hara's comment.) Study in his own library is backstopped with research at the Princeton University Library. "That's one of the reasons we moved to Princeton," he said. "I never went to college, but I've always wanted to live in a university town. I like to watch the athletics, and I like the feel of a good library nearby."

We asked Mr. O'Hara how he felt about the censorship difficulties that beset *Ten North Frederick* in Detroit and Albany last year. "The Detroit affair," he said, "was as disastrous to American letters as Korea was to the nation. The police out there said the book wasn't fit for sixteen-year-olds. Well, I don't write for sixteen-year-olds. The book had been out a year when they attacked the Bantam edition. They were not attacking the book itself but its availability. In Albany, I was the only recognized novelist included along with some smutty magazines. That was clever, lumping me in with them, and though they lost, it shows they're no fools tactically. Every little victory helps, of course, but first the courts have to determine what's smut and what's literature. I'm an honest artist. I've written fourteen books in twenty-four years and no one can accuse me of writing smut and make it stick. It's tough to determine where to draw the line on what's smut and what isn't, but I can't throw my hat in the air for joy at either the Detroit or the Albany decisions. The American Civil Liberties Union sat on its hands during both affairs, and the Authors Guild dragged its feet. The day I was indicted in Albany, I was on my way to New York to attend an Institute of Arts and Letters Dinner. A lawyer advised me that if I stayed in New York I might be jailed. So I wrote a note to the Institute explaining why I couldn't come and took the next train back to Princeton. The note was read at the dinner, but the Institute did nothing about the case. It should have."

Mr. O'Hara reads seven newspapers a day and a lot of magazines. He read no fiction during the two years he worked on *From the Terrace* and is not familiar with the work of younger novelists. In fiction, his preferences are Fitzgerald, Hemingway, Faulkner, and Sinclair Lewis, and he enjoys rereading their books. "It's not fair to the reader or to the author not to go back and reread—that's true of all the great writers. In *Babbitt*, I've found lots of stuff that I missed when it first came out. I get a great sense of rediscovery in rereading Fitzgerald, new aspects of style and nuance and hidden humor and wisdom. I'm not a poet and I don't read poetry. I think it's too restrictive a medium. All the values attributed to poetry—freedom and lyricism, for instance—are more true of prose than they are of poetry. Cummings, for example, is praised the most when he gets closest to prose."

Between reading and casual researching, Mr. O'Hara right now is resting and fooling around mostly, he says, and "wondering how stale I've got after writing eight hours a day for two years. I'll be fifty-four in January, and if I lived to be one hundred, I'd still have things to write about without ever having to leave Pennsylvania for a setting. There are several areas of the state's history—not modern areas, incidentally—that I'm interested in."

Right now, too, he's enjoying the excitement of having an important book about to be published. He likes the zip and the fun and the sense of accomplishment about a new book.

30 ✒ Mr. O'Hara

Lewis Nichols

A week from Thursday is Thanksgiving Day, by proclamation traditional to turkey and pumpkin pie, and by personal fiat publication day for John O'Hara. At least his new novel, *From the Terrace*, will come out that day, as did his last three years ago, *Ten North Frederick*. This is no coincidence. Mr. O'Hara is a practical man in a practical world.

"Thanksgiving Day is a holiday. You don't go to work. You get up maybe a little later than usual, and have time to read all of your paper—including the book reviews. Then, a couple of days after, come the Sunday papers—a

"Mr. O'Hara" by Lewis Nichols, *The New York Times Book Review* (15 November 1958), 8. © 1958 by The New York Times Company. Reprinted by permission.

chance to read other reviews on one big weekend. Then Monday—who knows?—you can stop off at a store on the way downtown and get the book."

Of the three years between big novels—*Ten North Frederick* had but 408 pages as against the newcomer's 897—Mr. O'Hara spent the last two writing "without interruption." This meant an eight-hour day, every day, although as usual the O'Hara day meant the night shift. The result of the concentration is that *From the Terrace*, scheduled for '59, will be coming in one Thanksgiving Day early. He finished in August, only now is "slowing down."

O'Hara books are noted for attention to detail—street addresses, minor historical events, the location of houses, restaurants, etc. He needs no school of researchers speeding about the country checking. Instead:

"I just remember obscure places and things, and test my memory every now and then when I'm trying to go to sleep. I'll take a street in Pottsville (Pa., and his hometown) and try to remember everyone who lived on it. The refinement is to try and remember the kind of car each family had. I can do it, too."

Future work? "I have material for some five novels I could write without once leaving the house." The long, narrative poem which has been in the O'Hara future book for years? "Still there, mapped out in my mind, about a guy who sang in a band. All I have to do is sit down and write it." Will there be anything more about Pal Joey? "No." Any private regrets for the passing of the lusty, earlier days of O'Hara?

"When Benchley died, the party was over."

31 ✒ Appt. With O'Hara

Rollene Waterman

John O'Hara lives in a white brick house along a country road in Princeton, New Jersey, with his thirteen-year-old daughter, Wylie, his wife, and a golden retriever named Pat. He wears tweedy jackets, walking shoes, and drives his open MG at a fast clip along rural lanes. Country squire during the daytime, O'Hara is a conscientious craftsman by night. He writes from midnight until dawn in a study filled with dictionaries, encyclopedias, and souvenirs of the past—John Held sketches of racoon-coated collegians, original illustrations for Fitzgerald's *Tender Is the Night*, and cartoons from former *New Yorker* colleagues. A small plaque is a reminder of the 1955 National Book Award which he won for *Ten North Frederick*.

In his checkered writing career, O'Hara has also collected a good many labels. He has been called a "barndoor writer," "hard-boiled author," and "a social commentator with a semi-snobbish point of view." As a boy in Pottsville, Pennsylvania (population 25,000), O'Hara lived on a farm, well stocked with five cars and five ponies. His father was a leading local surgeon and John was provided with all the proper accoutrements of a socially-qualified young man. When his father died, the O'Hara fortunes changed swiftly—no ponies, no farm, and no Yale for John. He went to work for a time on the local newspaper, bitterly begrudging his former classmates their college educations. "I went on the bum," recalled O'Hara. "I traveled out West, worked on a steamer, took a job in an amusement part. I wanted even then to be a writer." He had read Owen Johnson's Law-

Rollene Waterman, "Appt. With O'Hara," *Saturday Review*, 41 (29 November 1958), 15. Reprinted with permission.

renceville stories, identified himself with Tarkington's Penrod, and found his mentor in Scott Fitzgerald. "I was fascinated," he said, "by the small-town boy in the Ivy League world."

Eventually he came to New York, where he worked on newspapers and magazines. He was rewrite man, football editor, drama critic, religious writer, for *Time*, the *New Yorker*, the *Herald Tribune*, and half a dozen others. These were his hard-drinking days and no job lasted long. In 1933 he began to work on his first novel, using his bed for a desk. "When I got down to my last three dollars I wrote to Harcourt, Brace. They liked the chapters I sent them and paid me fifty dollars a week for six months until I finished it." *Appointment in Samarra* was an immediate success and Hollywood offered him a lucrative job as a scriptwriter.

For O'Hara the decade of the thirties was a time of high living. He divided his time between Hollywood and New York, where as man-about-towns, he kept a couple of cars, a chauffeur, and duplex bachelor digs not far from his favorite nightspot, "21." He wrote *Butterfield 8*, created the irrepressible Pal Joey, and worked on now-forgotten movie scripts. War came and O'Hara went off to the Pacific as a correspondent.

"My writing took an upward turn after *A Rage to Live* in 1948," said O'Hara. "When I wrote my earlier books, like *Appointment*, I was in the farm clubs trying out for the Yankees. It was written from personal experience and emotion. As the years passed I matured and learned more about writing a novel. In *Rage* I set difficult technical tasks for myself and in *From the Terrace* they are even more difficult. Handling over a hundred characters in different times and at different places is a job in literary logistics. I don't rewrite and I don't outline. Newspaper work taught me to get it right the first time."

From his newspaper experience he learned to be a

stickler for accuracy. In gathering material for *From the Terrace* he talked to anyone who had useful facts— bankers, lawyers, Navy men, flyers—and wrote dozens of letters to verify the smallest detail. He has countless responses to his queries for information about planes in World War I, the inner workings of Wall Street, the precise wording on a U.S. Navy death notice.

Admittedly O'Hara is pleased with his new novel. "It's the best thing I've done. The scope of it—fifty years of our country's most exciting history—is larger than anything I've tried before. Writing this novel demanded more wisdom, more patience, more craft, all of which comes from growing older," said O'Hara, who is fifty-three. "I thought about *From the Terrace* for six years. It took me two years to write it. I feel I completed what I set out to do."

32 ✄ Talk With the Author

John O'Hara is fifty-three. As a younger man he was noteworthy as a participating expert on the night life of New York and Los Angeles. For the better part of ten years now he has led an industrious and quietly social life, centered at homes in Princeton, N.J., and Quogue, N.Y.

On the western outskirts of Princeton he has built a whitewashed-brick dwelling, suggesting a French manor house, where he lives with his wife, Katharine, and his daughter by his previous wife, who died in 1954. There, recently, he talked to *Newsweek* about his inward and outward working processes.

Newsweek, 52 (1 December 1958), 93–94. Copyright 1958 by Newsweek, Inc. All rights reserved. Reprinted by permission.

"Each of my major and chief minor characters," he said, "is usually based on a psychological pattern suggested by the life of someone I have known. In drawing from him I may take him out of his time, change him a great deal superficially, and displace him socially. Julian English, for instance, the socially correct hero of *Appointment in Samarra*, was drawn from a young man who actually lived on the other side of the tracks. Alfred Eaton is drawn from someone who isn't even an American. Sometimes I try to imagine what my basic character model would have been like if certain important things in his real life hadn't happened. That was the case with Joe Chapin of *Ten North Frederick*.

"With these basic patterns, I have the feeling that I know where the story is going to end. In a general sense, I can't go wrong, because I can't deviate from a line of life which is, in effect, rigidly set.

"In working out the details of the story I'm careful not to use anything which will be inconsistent with what will happen seven hundred pages ahead. And once I sit at the typewriter, I do very little ad-libbing. In writing *From the Terrace*, with a hundred characters and fifty years to cover, I used three written aids. I had an overall chart, placing the major characters, and those close to them, in time— what they were doing when. Then there was a journal I kept called 'So Far,' in which I noted down the events I'd covered, and there was a notebook my wife kept with pages for each character and a record of his appearances where, and in what connection.

"For two years I was at the typewriter five or six nights a week. I never started before midnight [O'Hara is a dedicated daytime sleeper]. Before that, I often watched TV, and recently I've been particularly fond of old English movies. After midnight, I wrote on the average for five hours. I don't make changes, I write right along, and often I get into a definitely rhythmic feeling about it. One night

I wrote for eight hours straight without getting out of the chair. I like to quit, as Hemingway says he does, when I'm going well and there is a momentum built up which will help me start off the next night. I'm also apt to get a physical warning signal, a pain across the small of my back related to exhaustion."

While writing a novel, O'Hara reads no new fiction. He does reread old favorites, such as Hemingway and Fitzgerald, and sometimes discovers new old favorites—one of the most recent has been *Robinson Crusoe*. He is already planning another long Pennsylvania-based novel. He sees no reason why he should abandon Pennsylvania, which he knows so thoroughly and regards as a social microcosm reflecting the entire United States.

On a recent trip to Hollywood, in connection with *From the Terrace*, he negotiated with Twentieth Century-Fox a tentative contract (dependent on legal arrangements) which would bring him $100,000 plus 25 percent of the profits for a film based on the novel, and $50,000 plus 25 percent for each sequel or remake. The scale of the book would easily seem to permit such a program.

33 ✒ Reply to Questionnaire

Dear Mr. Ruas:

I reply as follows to the items on your questionnaire:

1. Alfred Eaton, from your latest novel, attended Princeton, as did several other characters from previous works. Why did you choose Princeton?

From "Appointment With O'Hara," by Robert A. Burt and Charles E. Ruas, *The Daily Princetonian* (7 January 1959), 2. Permission to reprint this interview was granted by The Daily Princetonian Publishing Co. The title has been supplied by the editor. Question 14 was omitted from the published interview.

Mr. O'Hara: Why not Princeton?

2. Do you feel that the education received at Princeton shapes your characters in a particular way; if so, what?

Mr. O'Hara: No, as to education. Until about 1930 Princeton did produce a fair number of graduates or near-graduates who had the same style in clothes, the social graces, and even an attitude toward the world, but that is no longer true.

3. Why do you write?

Mr. O'Hara: What a question! Because I want to.

4. What do you conceive to be your personal role as a novelist in American society?

Mr. O'Hara: My personal role as a novelist in American society is that of John O'Hara, a novelist.

5. What do you think is your responsibility to, your message for this generation?

Mr. O'Hara: I have no responsibility to or message for this generation.

6. Does the novelist have an impact on his generation?

Mr. O'Hara: The novelist has an impact on his generation to the degree that he may influence a few members of his generation and those few may influence a few others.

7. Is there a place in society for the Novelist?

Mr. O'Hara: There is a place in society for everybody.

8. Does the *Saturday Review* do justice to your work by calling you a social historian?

Mr. O'Hara: I am, second, a social historian; I am, first, a novelist. Every good novelist is a social historian.

9. Does this limit the message of your works specifically for this generation?

Mr. O'Hara: See Answer 5.

10. What do you feel are the main trends in American society?

Mr. O'Hara: The main trends in American society are in

the direction of Washington, D.C., crying for federal aid to everything, and a refusal to believe that temporary "security" is not worth the price of the monster of centralized government.

11. Are you personally in sympathy with these trends?
Mr. O'Hara: Hardly.

12. Do the conflicts of your characters stem from an alienation from the main trends of society?
Mr. O'Hara: This question should be simplified.

13. In creating a character, do you use specific people as models or do you use typed traits?
Mr. O'Hara: So should this; I do not understand what you mean by "typed traits."

15. Whom do you think is our greatest living writer?
Mr. O'Hara: That word should be who, not whom. Nominative case.

16. Do you think that commercial considerations distort what you are trying to do or say?
Mr. O'Hara: Nothing distorts what I try to say. I say it.

17. What does the fact that all your novels have made the best-seller list signify?
Mr. O'Hara: It signifies that a lot of people buy my books.

18. Why do you think that people feel *Appointment in Samarra* has never been surpassed in your subsequent writings?
Mr. O'Hara: That is no longer the case.

19. Why have you chosen to write about a particular social group?
Mr. O'Hara: This question reveals a limited knowledge of my work.

20. Why are all your main characters charming but unexceptional?
Mr. O'Hara: See Answer 19.

21. What do you feel is the role of the exceptional person in American Society?

Mr. O'Hara: The role of the exceptional person in American society is usually miscast.

22. It has been said that your characters lead empty, almost futile lives—is this inherent in them as humans, or in the society?

Mr. O'Hara: Oh, dear.

23. In the light of your emphasis on physiological details in describing sexual relationships, do you feel that love is divorced from sex?

Mr. O'Hara: Do you feel that physiological details have been divorced from sex?

24. You consciously realize that your characters' main flaw is an inability to love. Why is this a flaw rather than a strength?

Mr. O'Hara: I realize no such thing.

Yours, truly,

John O'Hara

34 ✍ Good Writers Get Published
John O'Hara

As a professional author, one who makes his living entirely by writing for money, my first answer to your request for comment on the NBA is that I was the last to win the fiction prize before it carried a $1,000 cash value. It would be nice if cash awards were made retroactively to those of us who missed out. . . . I never had won any-

Maurice Dolbier, "What NBA Means to Some Past Winners," *New York Herald Tribune Book Review* (1 March 1959), 2. Reprinted with permission of I.H.T. Corporation © New York Herald Tribune. The title has been supplied by the editor.

thing for my novels and short stories. . . . I happen to know that two of my novels were up for the Pulitzer Prize, but I never got it. So the NBA was especially gratifying to me. . . . I do not go along with the idea that the Awards should ever be made to "a somewhat unknown writer." (This is not the same thing as saying it should go only to writers of best sellers.) Considering the wholly professional character of the sponsorship of the NBA, I believe that it should be the duty of the NBA jury to reward the all-out professional author, and not to dig around and rescue a writer from obscurity. . . . In this country the good writer does get read. As I have said before *Sweet and Sour* I don't believe that there are better writers than Hemingway, Steinbeck, Faulkner, Cozzens and I pining away in Brown County, Ind., or in the espresso joint on Third St., or on the faculty of East South Dakota A. & M. Good writers get published, and they then cease to be "somewhat unknown."

35 If You're Going to Write, Nothing Will Stop You

John O'Hara

Creative writing, or literature, comes from all sorts of people and all sorts of places; so I do not rule out the possibility that it may come from a creative writing course. But there really is no shortcut to good writing, and no way to learn it except to write. If my daughter, now fifteen, should want to write, I would urge her not to take a creative writing course. The time would be better spent

Copyright © 1961 by La Salle College. Originally published in *Four Quarters*, 10 (January 1961), 17. John O'Hara's reply to a request from La Salle College in Philadelphia for a contribution to a symposium on the teaching of creative writing. The title has been supplied by the editor.

in Latin or Greek, French or Russian; or in history or physics or in political economy or in philosophy.

The word *creative* seems to contradict the idea of writing as a teachable art. The word *valid* . . . also disturbs me. Valid is one of the most misused words in modern jargon. It is an egghead favorite and almost never correctly used. It is one of those words like *dichotomy*, *denigration*, *ambivalence*, and God knows how many others that I consider show-off words. Instead of trying to teach "creative" writing, students should be taught how to spell and to respect the language. How many creative writing students can use *who* and *whom* correctly? . . .

Most students who want to be writers are looking for a life of undisciplined ease, and the product of creative writing courses proves it. If you're going to write, nothing will stop you, but writing is strictly a do-it-yourself enterprise.

36 ✎ A Writer's Look At His Town, Career, and Future

Kenneth D. Munn

John O'Hara was talking about the "new O'Hara," the quieter, mellowed O'Hara who many say has changed more than a little from those hell-raising days in the twenties and thirties when the "old O'Hara" was the nightclubbing companion and elbow-bending buddy of practically everybody who was called somebody.

The Princeton Packet (23 November 1961), 1, 4. Mrs. O'Hara selected John O'Hara's statement in this interview for his epitaph: "Better than anyone else, he told the truth about his time, the first half of the Twentieth Century. He is a professional; he wrote honestly and well." Permission to reprint this interview was granted by The Princeton Packet, Inc.

He doesn't deny that middle age has something to do with it. "As I remarked once before, 'The party was over when Benchley died.' That was in 1945. After that I was good and ready to leave New York and California where I had spent most of my mature life.

"But the real break came . . . " He paused, then went on. "I nearly died eight years ago. My doctor told me I'd better take care of myself. So eight years ago I went on the wagon. . . . Now I take care of myself."

John O'Hara at fifty-six is a broad six-footer trimmed down to around 185 pounds, thanks to a steady diet and "walking a lot." His voice is low, tough-sounding, with a straight-from-the-shoulder edge like a veteran traffic cop who has been around a while and tolerates no nonsense.

Mr. O'Hara intensely dislikes being photographed, dislikes maybe a little less being interviewed or meeting new people, but will. He has a cosmopolitan courteousness and a remarkable memory which can pinpoint not only people, but times and places. And he listens as intently as he speaks, an intensity broken only by an occasional smile that starts somewhere around the eyes.

Sitting in his study at "Linebrook," named by him after Prettybrook and Province Line Roads which border it, he was talking now about his new book, his first collection of short stories since *Hellbox* in 1947. The new book of twenty-six short stories, *Assembly*, will be published tomorrow, Thanksgiving Day, by Random House.

"I'm writing so much I'm overtaking myself," he said, smiling briefly. This will be his third book since last Thanksgiving. The others were *Five Plays* and three novellas, *Sermons and Soda-Water*. He is now at work on a "big novel, about two-thirds finished," to be called *The Lockwood Concern*. "It won't be ready for quite a while," he said.

And just like money in the bank, he has two other novels completed and tucked away in a safe. Although he has picked no release date for his next book, it will "definitely be a novel."

One of the completed novels, *The Big Laugh*, concerns an actor who becomes a movie star during the "mid-talkies" and the other is about a "mythical college town in Pennsylvania" during the thirties, forties, and fifties.

Discussing a real college town in New Jersey, Mr. O'Hara said he was "interested in Princeton without participating." As an example, he has no interest in local politics, "other than in voting, which I do conscientiously." He continued, "I came here as a Democrat, but I switched about eight years ago to a Republican," explaining, that "as you grow older, you tend to grow more conservative."

The O'Haras moved here in 1949 to escape the dust-laden New York City air to which their only child, Wylie, had become allergic.

Why Princeton? "We wanted to move to a college town. We looked at Swarthmore and at New Haven, but that was out because of the dreadful weather." He said they picked Princeton because of its "excellent library facilities, its sports, and closeness to either New York or Philadelphia."

"I like a college town because there's no 'keeping up with the Joneses.' The pace—the economic level of the town—is set by the full professors. This is also a very rich town, but there is not a great deal of conspicuous spending, as in Glen Cove, L.I., for example. I visited Princeton quite frequently during the twenties and thirties. I was writing sports then and also had friends here, so I knew the town."

What about Princeton today?

"Till World War II, the principal industry was the university. It still is, but around the time I moved here it was ceasing to be 'university town.' First year or two after we moved here I couldn't walk along Nassau Street without meeting one or two people I knew, or take a train to New York from Princeton Junction without meeting one or two people on the platform. I never failed to meet somebody I knew. Now there are times when I don't see anyone.

"I don't like to see Princeton lose the character it has had for many decades. I don't like to see Princeton become absorbed in that long populated thoroughfare between Boston and Washington, which is rapidly becoming one long contiguous residential area. Nothing to be done about it, I guess. There's little any one man or municipality can do about it. It's growth, but growth doesn't always mean progress."

The talk then switched to the mementos nearly filling the O'Hara study. Memory-prodding photographs are everywhere.

There is a photograph of late, great humorist and long-time O'Hara friend, Robert C. Benchley. He is standing with his arm tucked Napoleon-fashion into the long admiral's coat he is wearing. He is smiling proudly, loftily—despite the fact he is not wearing trousers. The understandable explanation, "That was at a party; he was tight."

And from another long-time O'Hara friend who recently died, James Thurber, a huge cartoon, measuring about four by three feet, framed and hung in the hallway near the writer's study.

The Thurber original, "a *New Yorker* rejection," shows a man standing, talking to another man. Behind them seated in a chair with her back toward them, is a woman gazing up rapturously at a violinist, intent on his playing. The first Thurber-man is saying to his friend, "I Wasn't Worried About My Wife When He Was A Writer."

Born in Pottsville, Pa., in 1905, Mr. O'Hara was the eldest of eight children. His five brothers and two sisters live in New Jersey, Pennsylvania, and New York. His father, a surgeon, attended the University of Pennsylvania, as did his brothers.

"There's my alma mater," commented Mr. O'Hara, pointing to a Columbia University plaque hanging on his study wall. "I took a course in history there once . . . My only college education."

A former reporter, engineer, boat steward, secretary in a briqueting plant, gas meter reader, freight clerk on the Pennsylvania Railroad, soda clerk, and picture press agent, he was also Heywood Broun's secretary, began writing criticism and features for newspapers, worked for both *Time* and *Newsweek* magazines, was editor-in-chief of the *Pittsburgh Bulletin-Index* and wrote screenplays. After his novel, *Appointment In Samarra*, was published in 1934 and became a success, he stayed with fiction writing.

His other successes include *Butterfield 8*, *Pal Joey*, *A Rage To Live*, and *Ten North Frederick*, which won the National Book Award, the only book award ever presented to Mr. O'Hara.

"It used to hurt, never winning an award," said Mr. O'Hara, who still considers *From The Terrace* his best novel, "but I've never been a pet of the intellectuals, the eggheads. I'm an extremely conscientious writer and I know my trade. When I write a novel I do a lot of digging. I was okay for good notices when a book came out, but not good for an award. I was nominated but never won. It used to hurt quite a bit."

Perhaps that's why Mr. O'Hara said he doesn't intend to write an autobiography. "Maybe if I live to be seventy I'll write one. I've got too damned much other work to do. Writing an autobiography is all right for a public official, it's almost his duty. But if I ever wrote an autobiography I'd have to level, and I wouldn't want to level while the people I'd be writing about are still alive."

But, in a mood befitting the "new" O'Hara, he said that

"it's very quiet here now. My wife has three grown children. My previous wife died . . . it will be seven years this January. My daughter is away at school. She's in her third year at St. Timothy's. Maybe once a month we have six or eight people for dinner. We almost never go to cocktail parties. It's wonderfully quiet."

And in this milder mood, John O'Hara was asked if he were a literary critic, how would he sum up the career thus far of John O'Hara the writer?

"Better than anyone else, he told the truth about his time, the first half of [the] Twentieth Century. He is a professional; he wrote honestly and well."

And John O'Hara is still writing honestly and well.

37 ✍ Don't Say It Never Happened
John O'Hara

A few weeks ago I had a letter from a retired professor of English at a land-grant university, a teacher who is practically unique in that he is also a friend of mine. Bill said he had seen a postgraduate piece about me, written by a former student of his. It was pretty bad, he said, but if I had any curiosity about it he would send it to me. He then quoted from the piece to show the kind of error he found in it, which was apparently much more about me than about my work. One of the errors, which Bill had reason to know was an error, was the statement that I was "mistaken" when I told an interviewer that my father had once owned five automobiles at the same time.

New York Herald Tribune Book Review (8 April 1962), 3. Reprinted with permission of I.H.T. Corporation © New York Herald Tribune. Angered by statements that his boyhood poverty dictated his choice of material, John O'Hara wrote this correction.

Well, my father did own five cars at the same time: three Buicks and two Fords. And anyone who wants to take the trouble can check on that fact. We had a six-cylinder Buick touring car, a four-cylinder Buick sedan, a four-cylinder Buick runabout, a Ford roadster, and another Ford roadster on the farm. We had a farm; 160 acres in the Panther Valley, shipping address, Cressona, Schuylkill County, Pennsylvania; but the thesis writer said that it was "doubtful" that the O'Haras ever owned a farm. My father was a member of the Jersey Cattle Breeders of America, and the chief distinction of the farm livestock was that we owned Noble of St. Mary's, a son of Noble of Oaklands, a Jersey bull of good lineage. We also had four mules, a team of sorrels, a bay carriage horse, a black carriage horse, five ponies (two of them registered Shetlands) and, for me, a five-gaited mare that my father purchased from the Kirby Horse Farm in Bowling Green, Kentucky.

My father, who had *not* worked his way through the University of Pennsylvania Medical School, made quite a lot of money in his day, for his day, but like many doctors he had no real business sense. However, you couldn't tell him that. He had made some money in the stock market, on Wells-Fargo and Bosch Magneto shares, and he was convinced that Germany would make a financial comeback in 1919. Consequently, when he died, intestate, and his safety deposit box was opened, it was found that he had bought a large amount of German marks, and they were absolutely worthless. He may have been a good surgeon, but in money matters he was a fool.

Now all this, and more of the same, is known to quite a few senior citizens of Pottsville, Pa. There are a lot of people my age and older who can recall that my father was a member of the Pottsville Assembly (I never was; I attended the Assemblies, but I was never a member); that we had a family membership in the old Outdoor Club, which was a great deal more exclusive than its successor, the Schuylkill Country Club; and there may even be a few old-timers who recall that my father, before he was married, lived at the Pottsville Club. I learned to read and write at Miss Katie's; I learned to dance at the Misses Linder's and at Miss Charlotte Brooks' and Miss Marie Hill's dancing classes. When we went to Philadelphia we stopped at the Bellevue, and we charged things at Wanamaker's and Strawbridge's, except my pumps, which came from Steigerwalt's. I had a coonskin coat before I was twenty, and every once in a while I hear from someone who recalls me as a dashing figure on horseback, booted and spurred and stuck-up.

Oh, we had it, all right . . . for a while. It is easy enough to second-guess my old man in financial matters, and I wasted a lot of time doing just that after he died. I was the oldest of eight children, and when he died I had just started work as a newspaper reporter, salary $6 a week. For a while my mother tried to keep up appearances, which she did by selling bonds she had inherited from grandpa, but they didn't last very long, and we had to get out of the country club and, after my next sister, none of the younger children could go away to boarding-school. We were really strapped, and I was no help at all. We had some rich relatives who could have done something for the younger children (not for me; I already had a reputation as a wild one), but they decided that the Lord would provide. And we found that it is almost impossible to collect money that is owed to a dead doc. So I went from professional-class security to near poverty almost literally overnight.

This—I assure you—accurate if somewhat depressing financial statement is also inspired by another, more recent piece than the postgraduate's thesis. I have just been reading a piece about me by a man whom I shall call

George Sump. Mr. Sump is a member of the Literary Establishment, that self-perpetuating, self-sustaining group of eggheads, "fellowship bums," academicians, and politicians of arts and letters, who hate me. And they better, for I despise them. Mr. Sump has put together a clip-book, 513 pages long with index, in which he naturally takes me to task for writing 900-page novels, that cost "almost seven dollars" (Mr. Sump's clip-book, sent to me free by the publisher, is priced at $7.50). I am subjected to the usual abuse that I have been taught to expect from the Literary Establishment, the Standard Operating Procedure that raises two questions: don't they read each other? And, don't they read anyone else? It is the same kind of abuse, in pretty much the same wording, that I have been getting for twenty-eight years come August, and it is pretty tiresome. I can read it, like a lawyer, down the middle of the page. The only time I pause is when I once again encounter a reference to me as a boy from "the wrong side of the tracks."

Most boys from the wrong side of the tracks are for that very reason practically guaranteed the sweet treatment by the Sump-type of critic. For me they make an exception, and I wonder why. I must have read at least a dozen articles about myself that set out to prove that I had never had a banana split until I was able to afford "21." A couple of years ago a local herring-wrapper devoted a whole week, a full page a day, to create an image of me as a lush, a sex maniac, a social climber, and a boy from the wrong end of the right street, like having a 2000-number on Park Avenue. Those pieces always imply, or simply state, that I got the country club atmosphere for my first novel (which I wrote when I was twenty-eight years old) while pressing my nose against the club windows from the outside, or burying the same beak in the society pages of the *Pottsville Journal*.

The fiscal-sociological details that I have provided in this article have always been available to reporters, and the curious thing is that the juicier details of my early life are more likely to be found in the country club area. I read in one article that I was a pool shark, which would have got guffaws from old friends who know that my all-time high run was twenty-six balls. I once turned down an offer to be a bootlegger, but the offer was made only because at the time I was still a member of the country club. I have been on the bum, I have been a ship's steward, a park guard, a day laborer, a switchboard operator, and a managing editor, in my pursuit of the essential buck. I once went three days without anything to eat and only tap water to drink, and once in Chicago I braced a guy for a quarter and he turned me down because he said I was wearing a Brooks suit (which was quite true). The fact that I had no overcoat and that it was November cut no ice with him, the jerk. Oh, I have been poor.

But I wonder why the Sump types and their investigators are so anxious to place me so firmly on the wrong side of the tracks from the earliest beginnings? As a matter of fact, speaking of tracks, one of my cousins owned a private car; and when I was about twelve years old I had a ride with Mr. and Mrs. Stotesbury in their private varnish, as Mr. Beebe calls it.

Lay off, Sumps. In 1918, in a store on Chestnut Street in Philadelphia, my old man bought me a pair of riding boots for $55 and the first pair of wing-tip brogues I had ever seen, for $26.50. He paid cash, and we didn't have to thumb it home. That didn't last, but don't say it never happened.

38 ✍ I Have Recently Been Putting Action Back Into My Stories
John O'Hara

"In the past thirty or forty years there have been very few first-rate short stories that contained action or plot," John O'Hara has told the *Post*. "We who wrote the stories have been influenced by Chekhov, among others, and have been reacting against the junky plot stories that many mass-magazine fiction editors used to insist upon. That reaction was OK. The so-called 'popular' plot stories did bear little relation to truth and life. But having been one the the leading practitioners of the oblique and plotless, I have recently been putting action back into my stories. 'The Lawbreaker' is in this genre. I want *Post* readers to be constantly surprised. I do not want them to think they know what to expect when they see my name on a story."

This passage from John O'Hara's letter to Don Schanche was printed as a headnote to "The Lawbreaker," *The Saturday Evening Post*, 236 (16 November 1963), 53. The title has been supplied by the editor.

39 ✍ The World, I Think, Is Better Off That I'm a Writer
Arthur Pottersmann

Mr. John O'Hara, the American writer who takes skeletons out of the family cupboard and turns them into mighty novels, arrived in England last night accompanied by his new Rolls-Royce.

London Sun (21 September 1965), 3. Reprinted with permission of Syndication International, Ltd.

He is here with his wife and twenty-year-old daughter for a month's tour of England, Scotland, and Ireland—and to talk business.

His latest novel, *The Lockwood Concern*, has just been bought by an American paperback firm for £170,000, and Mr. O'Hara will find one British firm eager to pay more than £20,000 for the British rights.

I talked with John O'Hara, a tall, heavily-built man, with icy blue eyes, as we sailed in the Queen Mary into Southampton last night. He speaks quietly but emphatically, and with rare bursts of laughter.

He has written a score of novels and several hundred short stories—everything from *Appointment in Samarra* and *Pal Joey* to family sagas. Though a near millionaire at sixty, he is still as prolific as ever, with a long novel, four novellas, and a volume of short stories completed in the last few years.

He told me: "I love writing. It comes easy to me, and hence my great output. Now that my energy isn't dissipated in drinking"—he went on the wagon after a haemorrhage twelve years ago—"I have enough to enable me to go on writing for as long as I live.

"I am a curiously religious man, in my own way. I was brought up a Roman Catholic, but I left that a long time ago. My talent may not have been God-given, but it is easy to think that it is, and if that is the case, then I owe something to that talent.

"The purpose of my writing? Well, I've been called a social historian, which is a rather fancy term but probably accurate enough.

"I want to have done—and to a large extent I have done—what someone like Dickens did in the nineteenth century.

"I am not over-modest about my work. I believe I can make a fairly objective appraisal of it.

"I disagreed with my father about becoming a writer.

He was an outstanding surgeon, I was the eldest of six sons and it just seemed to him an abdication not to study medicine.

"Long after he died, when I had my first success as a novelist, I thought quite seriously about becoming a doctor.

"I was twenty-nine then. I would have been a good doctor, but there are lots of good doctors, and not that many good writers. The world, I think, is better off that I'm a writer.

"Before I die, yes, I would like to receive the Nobel Prize—but that everybody wants. I have the Award of Merit of the American Academy of Letters—that is like your Order of Merit—and I'm reconciled to never getting the Nobel.

"I have never gone in for literary politics. I have never played that game. The people at literary cocktail parties have always bored me. If I wanted to get drunk, I did so on my own with my own choice of company.

"Am I cynical? Yes, I think so. There is a term I use for youth: 'the unearned cynicism of youth,' in other words, the beatniks, and near beatniks, who are sour and cynical without having earned the right through living to be so experienced.

"Cynicism isn't a necessary quality of having lived a long time. I'm sure the Pope isn't cynical.

"I have had a very harsh time of life, disappointments, and so forth. I have a lot of pain. I'm supposed to brace my back.

"But while I am having this pain, I can lose it in work or pleasure, writing or playing bridge. In other words, I can forget it although it is always there, sometimes very acutely, so I have to walk with a cane. Sometimes I cannot walk at all.

"Curiously enough, I think that most lives do balance out.

"I've had my joys and my tragedies. If you get the even break, that's all you have a right to expect on earth. I've come out fairly even. I have no real cause for complaints.

"I've been written off, physically and professionally, several times. I've learned as I got older not to demand too much.

"Now I have a lovely wife, a lovely daughter, a Rolls-Royce, and I don't spend all my time leaning on a cane.

"I can die tomorrow, and know that I have left some mark on the world. I can assure you that forty years ago you could have got very good odds that I would never do that."

40 ✒ John O'Hara . . . Two Blows He Had to Beat

Peterson Grosvenor

If sales figures and the appreciation of the reading public are anything to go by then John O'Hara is a giant among American novelists.

Ever since that so-brilliant first novel *Appointment in Samarra* he's sold by the multimillion.

Now, at sixty-two he looks back on twenty novels (*Butterfield 8*, *Pal Joey*, *From the Terrace*) and several hundred short stories.

But it's not always been a happy life and this week, on one of his rare visits to London, the portly, blue-eyed Mr. O'Hara let me in to some of the secrets of it.

"Ever since my first novel I've had a bad time with the critics, who reckon that nothing's been so good as my first book.

London Daily Express (4 May 1967), 6. Reprinted with permission of The Daily Express.

"It used to hurt. It only ceased to hurt about five years ago when I developed a tougher hide.

"I figured that a lot of it was sheer envy. The critic that really counts is yourself. I've always striven for the first rate. I sincerely believe that a lot of the time I've achieved it."

There was another, somewhat darker, period in O'Hara's life when, as he confessed: "I was dissipating all my energies in drink and high living. I was drinking a quart of whisky a day and that takes time—not just to drink, but to have your hangover and to get better from your hangover. It was a period when I couldn't write."

Then, fourteen years ago, O'Hara was hit by two deep blows, one a serious internal hemorrhage, the other, within months, the death of his second wife.

"My doctors warned me off drink on pain of death. When my wife died soon after and I had a young daughter to bring up, I knew I really had to."

Did he miss drink? "Yep," he said, sipping a glass of iced coke, "there are times when I miss it like hell. But I've never touched a drop since. I guess maybe I've found my substitute in work."

It would certainly seem like it. Among serious American authors there can be none more prolific than O'Hara. His themes, set against a background of moneyed middle-class American life, are universal ones—sex, power, and the inevitability of a man's fate.

He writes compulsively, and without effort, about eight hours a day.

"I'm mainly a night-bird: it's my old newspaper training. I was a rewrite man on the *Herald Tribune*. My journalistic training has been everything to me.

"A great novelist has to be a great reporter—the greater the reporter the greater the novelist. I'm there to set down the truths of our times as I see them, and that to me is even more important than providing entertainment to the reader."

He types all his books in just one draft; there is no rewriting, no repunctuation, almost no revising. He averages about one minor correction every two pages.

"I know what I want to say. My training as a rewrite man makes me get it right first time."

His latest novel, *The Lockwood Concern*, the frequently earthy chronicle of a rich American family is published today by Four Square Books at 10s. 6d.

We were lunching in his suite, No. 105 in Claridge's. I from a steak, he from two spartan-looking poached eggs. He was dressed in white silk pyjamas and a pink-checked dressing gown.

"I'm not a well man," he said. "I contracted a cold on the plane across so I shan't stir out of my suite.

"I've got a good deal wrong with me, including a congenitally bad back, persistent hypertension, and a hiatus hernia, which means your food sometimes goes the wrong way. It can kill you.

"It killed my friend Tommy Dorsey. So I've got to look after myself.

"But I'm no hypochondriac. I've swallowed my share of liquor, but there's something curious in my chemistry which makes me hypersensitive to pills. If I take tranquillizers I have to have a baby's dose. So now I don't use them at all."

He sounded gloomy and rather tired. But I suspect he gets some fun from life. Motoring is a big hobby. He runs three British cars—a Rolls-Royce, a Jaguar, and a 1948 MG—and his daughter has a Triumph Spitfire.

"British cars are sound economics," he declares, "and I'm not averse to the snob appeal. My good friend the governor of New Jersey has allocated me three fine registration numbers—JOH 1, JOH 2, and JOH 3."

For fuller show he sports five automobile club badges

on the Rolls radiator, including R.A.C. and A.A.—but not the American A.A. "There's no smartness in that."

Always, when he's wondering what to do with life, he turns to writing.

"I've got two novels going at the moment, one set in Indiana, the other in Pennsylvania. They'll both be finished before the end of the year.

"Haydn went on composing into very old age. Picasso went on painting long after he needed to. If you're a professional then you'll always want to create.

41 ✍ O'Hara, in Rare Interview, Calls Literary Landscape Fairly Bleak

Alden Whitman

John O'Hara gazed upon the American literary scene the other day and concluded, crustily, that it was a virtual wasteland.

The sixty-two-year-old novelist, short-story writer and playwright waived a long-standing rule against interviews to mark his 35th book. *The Instrument*, which will be published Thanksgiving Day by Random House. Mr. O'Hara, probably the most productive of living, serious writers, has averaged better than a book a year since his first novel, *Appointment in Samarra*, in 1934.

The setting was Linebrook, Mr. O'Hara's comfortable home on the outskirts of this college town, where he has lived since 1949. Seated in a padded swivel chair in his book-lined, memento and gimcrack-filled study, the writer pungently but gently ticked off his distastes.

"O'Hara, in Rare Interview, Calls Literary Landscape Fairly Bleak" by Alden Whitman, *The New York Times Book Review* (13 November 1967), 45. © 1967 by The New York Times Company. Reprinted by permission.

"I don't like any of them," he said of writers today. "You know what their stuff is before you open their books."

"They lack intimate knowledge of people," he added, drawing on one of the twenty-two cigarettes he consumed in a three-hour chat.

Mr. O'Hara, whose work is marked by a strong narrative thrust, psychological patterns, and character analysis, said that "young writers, those under forty and some over, haven't learned this business" of crafting fiction.

"I've never been able to read Norman Mailer," he said, tilting forward in his leather chair and cupping his massive head in his left hand. "Mailer is a dirty Saroyan."

Mr. Mailer, whose *Why We Are in Vietnam* was published this fall, is not a careful writer in Mr. O'Hara's view. Like those who want to be "instant Hemingways but they're not," Mr. O'Hara maintained, Mr. Mailer has neglected to master the basics of storytelling.

"Too many books now are judged on the basis of intent," he went on in a low pleasant baritone as he lit a cigarette taken from a tooled-leather box on his desk. "Bill Styron, you'd think *The Confessions of Nat Turner* was the book of the century.

"I don't think the book is that. Overpraise is ruinous to the guy who should be working his way toward big things. No one is going to be reading that book ten years from now!"

The trouble, Mr. O'Hara remarks, is that it is too easy nowadays for a young writer to be successful and make a lot of money without putting in an apprenticeship of observation and diverse writing, like Mr. O'Hara did as a newspaper reporter.

"Writers once had to earn a living," he declared with asperity. "Now there are these God damn foundations. Security must be made by yourself in our line of work."

Mr. O'Hara shrugged off James Jones, whose *Go to the*

Widow-Maker came out earlier this year, and he shook his head over Bernard Malamud, whose most recent novel is *The Fixer*.

"Malamud is writing about an extremely parochial world," he remarked, adding that this verdict also covered Saul Bellow, author of *Herzog*.

"They say great themes make great novels," Mr. O'Hara continued as he sipped a glass of milk. "That's so, of course, but what these young writers don't understand is that there is no greater theme than men and women. That's what it all comes down to."

That reminded Mr. O'Hara of William Saroyan, who now lives abroad. "Bill was always interested in men and women—the human being apart from Washington, Moscow, and the United Nations," he said. "Not all of his stuff was good, but some was good. He had heart."

Was there anyone Mr. O'Hara admired? He laughed. "James Gould Cozzens. Jim hasn't written much lately, but he is good. Another I admire is Thornton Wilder, one of our best, God knows!

"But Thornton's an excuse-maker for himself. He's one for the fleshpots. He's got a lot of money coming in and he makes excuses not to write."

Mr. Wilder's most recent novel, published earlier this year, is *The Eighth Day*.

Mr. O'Hara argued that self-discipline and a sense of ego were vital to literary greatness.

"I feel I owe something to my talent, which is damned close to a religion with me, close because maybe it is God-given," he continued, his voice rising. "By the time I was fifteen I knew all the rules and I certainly knew what I wanted to do. I wasn't going to be diverted by becoming a polo player (which I could have been, but I didn't have the money) or by taking other jobs. I knew I had to be what I've become.

"My circumstances are ideal now. I have a fine wife, a nice kid. I'm rich. I don't drink any more. I'm not diverted or distracted."

Possessing a well-organized fictive mind, Mr. O'Hara writes on a Remington Noiseless, working from midnight to 3 or 4 in the morning. His first draft is usually his last.

At the moment he is writing a comedy for the London theatre because "I want to do it just to have a play on in London before I die." The play is going very well, he said, and he expects to complete it by Christmas. A new collection of short stories, for publication next year, is already in manuscript, and he is a third of the way through "a big novel" that should be out in 1969.